Essential Tips for

504 Coordinators

Dr. NAKIA SIMMONS COTTON

DEDICATION

I want to honor and thank God, Jesus Christ, the head of my life. I also dedicate this book to my sons Kaylon and Kristian. Finally, I dedicate this book to the 504 coordinators in schools. Keep up the excellent work. (Philippians 4:13)

TABLE OF CONTENTS

ACKNOWLEDGMENTS

I thank my family for providing the guidance and ambition that have pushed me to strive for the best in life. You have supported me through prayers, love, and encouragement throughout every obstacle and opportunity. I dedicate this book to my father and mother, Hagmon Simmons and Valerie Williams (Willie). To my sons Kaylon and Kristian Cotton, the lights of my life and reasons for enduring, I hope to serve as your role model for patience and perseverance—my pushy but reassuring sister Katrina Williams. She told me to write a book and use my calling to help others. I want to remember my ancestors present in spirit, my guardian angels, Willie Mae Rogers, Lola Simmons, and Cassandra Simmons. Thanks to my friends and extended family from Tallahassee, Florida, to Metro Atlanta, Georgia. I am thankful for the countless other friends who have helped me grow, challenged me, and influenced my life.

I appreciate every good deed or obstacle because those challenges, critiques, and learning curves gave me the courage to rise above and propel me to this place.

Nakia ☺

CHAPTER 1

504 NEXT!

"Unless you try to do something beyond what you have already mastered, you will never grow." Unknown

When you see the number sequence 504, those not in the education field may think, "Oh, look at the time, or wow, 504 is a good number to play in the lottery." When educators see the number sequence 504, they may have different thoughts unrelated to the clock, a winning lottery number, or lucky numbers. The number 504 in education means federal laws, district policies, legal documents, and multiple meetings.

If you are reading this book, you are probably already familiar with the number 504, an abbreviation for Section 504 of the Rehabilitation Act. I am guessing that you are probably also familiar with the impact of Section 504 plans in schools and implementation for students with disabilities. The topic of Section 504 may be overwhelming and create a general feeling of uncertainty about compliance, federal laws, students with disabilities, paperwork, and policies in education.

As a fellow educator, I understand the feeling. I am currently a Section 504 Coordinator for a large district with 115 schools, where my sole responsibility is to ensure the implementation of Section 504 and other district-level leadership duties. Managing such a litigious position and other job duties, even in a perfect world, could foster feelings of anxiety due to the context of the subject.

School leaders and educators juggle many other responsibilities. With Section 504, school leaders and educators must write Section 504 plans, follow and monitor plans in the general education setting, support teachers, monitor compliance, ensure a Free and Appropriate Public Education, and collaborate with parents. Such responsibilities must be followed along with the possibility of the Office of Civil Rights intervening if something goes wrong or if a parent complains. I guess it does sound rather stressful and monumental when I address it from that viewpoint, but these are the facts. Section 504 may sound like something avoidable. However, avoidance is not an option, and neither is ignorance.

Section 504 is a growing trend in schools. As educators and leaders, we must adapt and learn to add this responsibility to our education duties, persevere, and overcome anxiety or avoidable feelings to work to level educational opportunities for students with disabilities. Section 504 is one of those federal laws that we must follow. Based on my experiences as a fellow educator and district Section 504 leader, I advise you to follow these federal mandates, provide services for students with disabilities, document appropriately, and adapt like we always do in education. The path of least resistance is best. Besides, we all want to provide quality, equitable learning experiences for all students.

I have always been involved with services with disabilities and Section 504 directly or indirectly throughout my education career. When I accepted my first position as a Special Programs Director at a Charter School, I initially learned about Section 504. I had managed to teach twelve years before I interacted with a 504 plan. Previously, I taught ESOL, special education, and at-risk learners, but I had never taught a student with a Section 504 plan. Yes, I had heard of 504 plans; however, they were beyond my world in education, mainly since I worked primarily in special education.

After working as the Special Programs Director, I became oriented and familiar with Section 504. While serving in this role, I had to educate, empower, and convince others to follow something unfamiliar. It was not special education but something with a plan, laws, and a Free and Appropriate Public Education. My thoughts were 504 what? What is that? Here goes another task that I must make the teachers implement. Why don't we offer an IEP? Isn't this the same as an IEP? Looking back, I realized that I had a lot to learn.

I did the Section 504 coordinator thing. I attended a Section 504 training with a local district and re-created that district's Section 504 training with updates for my district. I did what I was supposed to: deliver the professional development, provide teachers with the plan, and complete my checkboxes to maintain compliance. I had other duties such as special education, English Speakers of Other Languages, and Response to Intervention; however, I remained surface with Section 504 and completed my checkboxes to stay compliant.

While working in that role, I revised procedure forms and completed a systematic revamp of the Section 504 program since the information was outdated. However, special education, Child Study Team, and Response to Intervention occupied most of my time, and I could not dive deep into the 504 Coordinator role.

When you juggle various responsibilities, sometimes you get into survival mode and complete a task so you can get to the next job. The work gets completed, but it serves as a formality. That is usually the story of leadership and teaching based on some of my experiences. While serving as the coordinator, I advised and supported teachers only when a teacher requested assistance. I dealt with other duties; however, I managed Section 504 plans with the school counselors' support, who helped me manage the process. While working at the charter school, I learned the basics of Section 504. That was my first experience, but it certainly would not be my last.

Fast forward to my next position as a local school assistant principal. I relocated to Atlanta and worked as an administrator in charge of special education, RtI, ESOL, Science, Assessment, and Section 504 in a large metro school district. With my previous experiences, I was confident I was ready to conquer this job and whatever else came my way, including Section 504. I had presented webinars, led teams, and developed policies, programs, etc. I felt that those experiences as a special program director had prepared me for that position.

After navigating the waters in a new city, job, and environment, the newness and excitement began to fade into a rude awakening. The shiny new career move became an overwhelming place where I was again juggling. One of my duties was coordinating, managing, and monitoring Section 504 plans. Initially, I could do this again; I had done it before. How hard could this be? Within a brief span, the honeymoon was over, and all the duties I was responsible for, including 504, overwhelmed me. I began to reassess and wonder, "how am I going to manage 504 plans and lead others with all of these other duties?"

As a former educator, I knew there were a lot of functions

to school leadership. I witnessed school leaders in action through my "teacher lens." My past school leaders always maintained control, managed various duties, and supported teachers, parents, and students. I wanted to follow a similar path where I led Section 504 and other leadership responsibilities while impacting change and remaining compliant.

Going into the job, I was not naïve. I knew administrators worked hard but did not realize the extent until I worked in that position. I learned that my priorities would include leading and overseeing services for students with disabilities, supporting teachers, and working with parents.

I maintained a calm facade during the day, but I felt dread and anxiety once alone. I left the school every night after 6 pm and began job number two as a single parent. My two sons were home and needed love and attention. They were also adjusting to a new city and schools.

Instead of failing because failure was not an option, I had to figure out how to cope with duties effectively and ensure the 504 students received adequate services. I needed to prioritize and make a plan to juggle these precious litigious eggs and not drop them, make a mess, or end up with an egg on my face. I spent many sleepless nights balancing leadership, special education, and Local School 504 coordinator duties. I also was concerned and consumed with Section 504 compliance and asking myself questions such as:

- What is free and appropriate public education (FAPE)?
- Is this service legal and appropriate for a student with disabilities under Section 504?
- Are we compliant according to the Office of Civil Rights,

federal and state laws?

- Will we be sued?
- If we get sued, will I get fired?
- What does the Office of Civil Rights say about this topic?
- What is the "real" answer? I need a concrete solution!!
- What is the difference between Section 504 and Special Education?
- Are we serving and leading students with disabilities appropriately?
- Are we preparing students to advocate for themselves and overcome obstacles related to their disabilities?

A Section 504 coordinator's role is a form of leadership, whether you are a school leader, counselor, or work in another position. You lead since you are the appointed building Section 504 expert. In this position, others will come to you for Section 504 guidance and information. As a leader, counselor, or coordinator, your general job duties are to ensure compliant procedures, policies, and implementation of Section 504 in the building. Such a task can be a lot to absorb, particularly if you lack background knowledge in special education or Section 504, which services students with disabilities. The coordinator role can be overwhelming due to Section 504 policies, laws, and federal mandate requirements.

According to research from "Principals and Special Education: The Critical Role of School Leaders, "Many new building administrators find themselves suddenly thrust into situations in which they must be the final arbiter on matters related to strange-sounding issues such as IEPs, 504 decisions, due process hearings, and IDEA compliance" (CEC, 2001, p. 1)." The Critical Role of Leaders research confirmed my frame of mind when I began working in the position. I knew the district hired me to lead and cultivate academic success for students with disabilities; however, I felt suddenly thrust into a job and inexperienced, even with my previous special education and Section 504 background.

Principals and Special Education: The Critical Role of School Leaders states that administrators who clearly understand the needs of students with disabilities, IDEA, and the instructional challenges that educators who work with students with disabilities face are better prepared to provide appropriate support. Leaders that understand the importance of well-designed learning and working environments can facilitate the development of proper student placements and specialist assignments that accurately represent student needs." (DiPaola & Tschannen-Moran, 2003, p.9).

According to Civil Rights Collection data, in 2017-2018, 1.38 million students received services under Section 504. Based on an analysis of the data from The Advocacy Institute, 65% percent of those students who qualified identified as white, and 62.3% identified as male. The CRCD also reported that 47.7% of white students were eligible under IDEA, with 66.3% of those students identified as males. Data from 2017 reveals a substantial increase in special education students spending time learning among their nondisabled peers rather than separate from them. In fact, of those aged 6-21, 63.4% spend 80% or more of their time in general education classes. Based on those rising statistics, many students with disabilities will receive education with general education content teachers, and an increasing number will qualify for Section 504 services. (Mavis, 2022).

Due to the rapidly increasing numbers and the need for services, the Section 504 coordinator role is instrumental in promoting and protecting the students with disabilities in the local school building. There may never be an overnight formula other than your principal not assigning you to serve as the coordinator; however, that is highly unlikely, considering we all juggle duties in education. Unfortunately, there is also not a concrete blueprint for Section 504 coordinators. Every student is different. Therefore, you must align 504 practices supporting students' needs and differences. Thus, there is not a specific way to manage the role. Through various experiences, research, and training, we have learned to take knowledge and adapt it to our circumstances. Such experiences promote opportunities for evolution and growth.

All things take time, and we are all limited on time; however, following specific procedures, protocols, and tasks with due diligence saves time and some avoidable hardships. This book's rationale is to provide Section 504 knowledge, procedural insights, and Section 504 resources to support novice and veteran Section 504 Coordinators. I hope this book will provide information based on my personal and professional experiences with Section 504 leadership, serve as a general resource, and offer knowledge, tips, and tools to help empower and guide individuals in the Section 504 Coordinator role.

Here are some **Essential Tips** for getting started:

1. Identify your local district 504 coordinator(s) and save the district's page and resources.
2. Reach out to that coordinator to find out if there are trainings to attend.
3. Gain access to the documents or program where 504 plans are stored.
4. Find out where the 504 student records are for the students in your building.
5. Find a person or generate a report for all students in the building. You will need to start with the annual plan dates and the dates for the three-year periodic reevaluation.
6. Identify the feeder or schools similar and create a network with coordinators.
7. Identify your students with serious medical needs and high-maintenance parents. You may have to talk to your school nurse, administration, or that child's previous teachers.

"Leaders instill in their people a hope for success and a belief in themselves. Positive leaders empower people to accomplish their goals." Unknown

CHAPTER TWO
THE HISTORY OF SECTION 504

" The past haunts and the future taunts. This is particularly true if you love a child with special needs." ~ Lisa Thornbury

History provides valuable information about the past. It includes information about the perspectives and beliefs of our ancestors and others. Stearns (1998) explains that history helps us understand humanity, contributes to moral understanding, provides identity, shapes lives, and is essential for good citizenship. A recent article from Arcadia Publishing lists seven reasons for studying history. History helps us understand ourselves, others, and the world. History also teaches a working understanding of change, how to be reasonable citizens, and enables us to make better decisions. Finally, history allows us to create a new level of gratitude for everything (Why We must Study History, n.d.).

If you do not know where you are from, you will not know where you are going. Knowledge of history is essential if we plan to make future progress. It is always beneficial to learn the history of what you are doing to improve the job based on the historical connection, as stated by Stearns. With so many processes and ever-changing information to learn about Section 504, it is beneficial to know the historical context of Section 504. This chapter will give you some background on the evolution of Section 504 in America.

THE COMMENCEMENT OF SECTION 504

Individuals with disabilities have had many obstacles in life that, include exclusion and unequal treatment. The history of unequal treatment traces back to the 1800s; students with disabilities had few options during this time. Many students with disabilities were kept at home, or parents had to pay for private education. One of the first cases was in Massachusetts in 1893, where the Massachusetts Supreme Court upheld a student's expulsion based only on poor academic progress. The case Watson versus the City of Cambridge in 1893 expelled a student with a disability because the district determined that the child's mind was too weak to attend school and attain instruction. Rather than make accommodations, the district expelled the student. The next headline-making case was based out of Wisconsin thirty years later. The case Beattie versus Board of Education in 1919 denied education to a cerebral palsy student with facial contortions who drooled and had a speech impediment. The school claimed that the student's presence nauseated and depressed teachers, thus causing disruption and the school's need to remove the student (Smith, 2004).

"By the early 1900s, all the states had compulsory education laws, yet excluding children with disabilities was still widely practiced. "The educational rights of children with disabilities were gained largely through the efforts of parents and advocacy groups" (Yell et al., 1998, p.227). Section 504 addresses civil rights and equal opportunities; the first case to impact positive change for students with disabilities and equity originated from Brown vs. Board of Education in 1954. The Brown case determined segregation violated equal educational opportunities. The Brown decision became the turning point for race, gender, and disabilities, as this case emphasized that all people were entitled to a free and appropriate public education (Estes & Rao, 2008).

After the Brown Case in 1954, funding and rights increased for equity and inclusion for all students; however, schools still had the right to deny special education programs until the mid-1960s. Parent advocacy groups began to grow and advocate for students with disabilities. In 1961, President John F. Kennedy created The President's Panel on Mental Retardation. The panel's sanctions included federal aid to states. In 1965, the board took the initiative further, instrumental in developing the Elementary and Secondary Act that provided federal funding for public education.

The act was amended within a year to include the financing for Title VI, which added funding for grants for programs for children with disabilities. In 1973, Section 504 of the Rehabilitation Act was established, which stated that a person with a disability could not be denied or excluded from any program receiving federal financial assistance, private or public (Estes & Rao, 2008). Senator Hubert Humphrey, in 1977, declared Section 504 as: *"Section 504 of the Rehabilitation Act of 1973 (Section 504) is the civil rights declaration of the handicapped. It was greeted with great hope and satisfaction by Americans who have had the distress of physical or mental handicaps compounded by thoughtless or callous discrimination. These Americans have identified [Section] 504.*

With access to vital public services, such as education, they consider it their charter...it is a key to, and a symbol of, their entry as full participants in the mainstream of national life." (Senator Hubert H. Humphrey, Senate author of Section 504, Congressional Record, April 26, 1977, p. 12216)

Two years after the established Rehabilitation Act, about eight million people with disabilities were still excluded from public education or were inappropriately educated (Pulliam & Van Patten, 2006). Hence, the Education for All Handicapped Children Act, also known as Public Law 94-142, was signed by President Gerald Ford on November 29, 1975. The Education for All Handicapped Act focused on access to education but left the courts to determine the degree of educational opportunity. This law became the framework for future legislation (Yell et al., 1998). The act is now known as the Individuals with Disabilities Education Act (IDEA). The outcome was that now public education was a right and no longer a privilege for students with disabilities.

Throughout the years, Section 504 had to go through additional legislation to specify Civil Rights, what specific protections were offered, and who was eligible for those protections. The Education Amendments of 1974 amended Section 504 and, in 1978, clarified to explain the extent of civil rights and protections for persons with disabilities by including all the remedies, procedures, and rights contained in the Civil Rights Act of 1964 (Yell at. Al, 1998).

Section 504 was amended numerous times. There was still some ambiguity in Section 504 concerning the kind of protections for persons with disabilities. In 1978, Section 504 regulations were still unclear. The lack of action and ambiguity led to protests and sit-ins from advocacy groups and Department of Health,

Education, and Welfare (HEW) activities. In 1978, The Department of Health, Education, and Welfare published regulations after a federal court required HEW to disseminate regulations and after numerous demonstrations and protests at HEW offices (Brougher, 2010).

Section 504 was amended in 1978 and promised an equal opportunity system based on information from September 1973" (p. 47). *Section 504 states that no otherwise qualified handicapped individual in the United States... shall solely because of his handicap, be excluded from the participation in, be denied the benefits of, or be subject to discrimination under any activity receiving federal financial assistance.* (Section 504, 29 U.S.C. § 794(a)) Section 504 mandates aligned with the federal civil rights laws that prohibited discrimination by federal recipients based on race (Title VI of the Civil Rights Act of 1964) and sex (Title IX of the Education Amendments of 1972) (Brougher, 2010, p.2).

"These amendments expanded Section 504 nondiscrimination requirements to programs or activities conducted by executive agencies and added a new section which applied the remedies, procedures, and rights of Title VI of the Civil Rights Act of 1964 to Section 504 actions" (Brougher, 2011, p.2). The law also defined what a handicapped or what we now call a disabled person is described as: "A handicapped" person was defined as any person who has a physical or mental impairment that substantially limits one or more of that person's major life activities or a person who has a record of such an impairment, or a person who is regarded as having such an impairment" (Yell at al, 1998, p 224).

The primary purpose of Section 504 is to "prohibit discrimination against a person with a disability by any agency receiving federal funds. These agencies receive funds, personnel services, and property interests, whether receiving these benefits directly or through another recipient. Section 504 requires agencies that are the recipients of federal financial assistance to provide assurances of compliance, to take corrective steps when violations are found, and to make individualized modifications and accommodations to provide services that are comparable to services offered to persons without disabilities (Yell at al, 1998, p 224).

DISABILITY LAWS AND SECTION 504 IN SCHOOLS

The Education for All Handicapped Children Act, Public Law 94-142, is now known as the Individuals with Disabilities Education Act (IDEA). Let us explore and deepen our understanding of Public Law 94-142 and how it impacted Section 504. Numerous federal statutes, particularly the Individuals with Disabilities Education Act (IDEA), Section 504, and the Americans with Disabilities Amendment Act (ADAAA), address the rights of individuals with disabilities in education. Section 504 and the ADAAA intersect and significantly educate students with disabilities. There are some differences regarding K-12 schools. The Department of Education (ED) has construed the Section 504 compliance standards for schools to be the same as the basic requirements of IDEA (Brougher, 2011).

Public Law 94-142 has four purposes, according to the U.S.
Department of Education:

- "to assure that all children with disabilities have available
to them ... a free appropriate public education which emphasizes
special education and related services designed to meet their
unique needs
- to assure that the rights of children with disabilities and
their parents ... are protected
- to assist States and localities to provide for the education of
all children with disabilities
- to assess and assure the effectiveness of efforts to educate
all children with disabilities" (Education for All Handicapped
Children Act, 1975: Thirty-Five Years of Progress in Educating
Children with Disabilities Through IDEA, n.d., p.10).

Section 504 prohibits discrimination based on a disability.
The Office of Civil Rights enforces Section 504 in programs and
activities that receive federal funding. Recipients of federal
funding include public school districts, institutions of higher
education, and other state and local education agencies. The Office
of Civil Rights (OCR) is a component of the U.S. Department of
Education that enforces Section 504 of the Rehabilitation Act of
1973 and Title II of the Americans with Disabilities Act of 1990
(Title II). Title II prohibits discrimination in state and local
government services, programs, and activities (including public
schools) regardless of whether they receive any federal funding
(Protecting Students with Disabilities, n.d.).

The Americans with Disabilities Act Amendments Act of
2008, now titled (Amendments Act), effective January 1, 2009,
amended the Americans with Disabilities Act of 1990 (ADA) and

included a compatible amendment to the Rehabilitation Act of 1973 (Rehabilitation Act) that affects the meaning of disability in Section 504. The Title II regulations are applicable to free appropriate public education issues. However, Title II does not provide greater protection than relevant Section 504 laws.

The Office of Special Education and Rehabilitative Services (OSERS), a U.S. Department of Education component, administers the Individuals with Disabilities Education Act (IDEA). This statute funds special education programs. Each state educational agency is responsible for administering IDEA within the state and distributing the funds for special education programs. IDEA is a grant statute that attaches many specific conditions to receiving Federal IDEA funds. Section 504 and the Americans with Disabilities Act are antidiscrimination laws and do not provide any funding.

Section 504 regulations require school districts to provide a "free and appropriate public education" (FAPE) to each qualified student with a disability in the school district's jurisdiction, regardless of the nature or severity of the disability. "Under Section 504, FAPE consists of the provision of regular or special education and related aids and services designed to meet the student's individual educational needs as adequately as the needs of nondisabled students." An appropriate education for a student with a disability under Section 504 could consist of education in regular classrooms, education in regular classes with supplementary services, and special education and related services" (Protecting Students with Disabilities, n.d.)

Section 504 regulatory provision 34 C.F.R. 104.35(b) requires school districts to evaluate students individually before classifying a student as having a disability or providing special education services. The determinations are made through a multidisciplinary approach through a review of a variety of sources of data. The law is not specific as to the required team members. Section 504 Teams may consist of teachers, parents, counselors, nurses, administrators, and district personnel. Team members can usually provide valuable information, discuss the impairment, and assess the student's impairment in the learning environment (US Department of Education, 2020).

The team convenes with the parent and determines if the student has a "substantial limitation" to a major life activity. Once the team determines a "substantial limitation." The team will decide if the students require accommodations and modifications in a Section 504 plan to "level the playing field" with other general education peers, providing a Free and Appropriate Public Education (FAPE). The Section 504 plan serves as the blueprint for student services under Section 504. The plan may accommodate and modify the environment, instruction, or curriculum.

Section 504 plans are not special education-related, and services are provided in the general education environment. Students who qualify or are deemed eligible under a Section 504 plan are protected against discrimination and discipline. The team will need to determine if discipline infractions that cause a "significant change in placement" are related to the disability (Protecting Students with Disabilities, n.d.).

CURRENT TIMES AND PROGRESSION

By 1997, additional amendments were enacted to provide meaningful and measurable programs for all students (Hardman & Nagle, 2004). The Americans with Disabilities Amendment Act (ADAAA) and the Office of Civil Rights require compliance of school districts that receive federal aid. Those significant components include parent involvement, procedural safeguards (a systematic 504 process), evaluation, and due process.

According to the US Department of Education, Section 504 requires districts to notify parents regarding evaluation and placement decisions about their child. Under those rights, districts must inform parents of their right to review educational records and appeal any decision regarding evaluation and placement through an impartial hearing (US Department of Education, n.d.).

Parental rights and involvement are essential to Section 504. Parents are afforded rights under Section 504. The district should offer parents Section 504 rights at every Section 504 meeting. Parent rights confirm the evolutionary shift from the early days when parents and students with disabilities did not have any rights.

Section 504 parental rights are not as long as special education rights; however, as the Section 504 Coordinator, you should familiarize yourself with the basics to be knowledgeable and prepared. Also, know your district's due process and compliance procedures. The Local Education Agency Representative offers the final decision of FAPE. You will most likely serve as the Local Educational Agency Representative who will provide a Free and Appropriate Public Education on behalf of the district. Usually, districts have compliance manuals to support this process. Understanding the policies will equip you when faced with such decisions. Keep a copy of this manual as a blueprint.

Currently, other educational initiatives, such as IDEA 2004, align with the No Child Left Behind Act. These programs have enhanced special education at the state level, heightened accountability on state assessments, and emphasized "highly qualified teaching." Additionally, Response to Intervention is in conjunction with IDEA 2004.

Response to Intervention (RtI) is the "practice of providing high-quality instruction along with interventions matched to student need, monitoring progress frequently to make decisions about changes in instruction and goals and applying data to make important educational decisions" (NASDE, 2006). RtI is a general education initiative; however, the purpose was to change struggling students' educational access and promote interventions through leveled tiers to address learning gaps and behavior, reducing over-identification of special education referrals in schools (Estes & Rao, 2008).

In schools today, Section 504 has become a pressing issue with continuous growth and awareness. Section 504 has also become a legal battlefield in many ways, with many due process hearings, letters from the Office of Special Education Programs (OSEP), Supreme Court rulings, and landmark cases that have redefined federal laws and regulations. Various organizations and groups now support the parents and educators of Section 504 throughout the country.

Some of those groups include:

- Children and Adults with Attention Deficit Disorder
- Learning Disabilities Associations
- ADA Disability Rights Information (U.S. Department of Justice)
- Alliance for Technology Access (ATA)
- American Association of People with Disabilities (AAPD)
- (The) Center for Appropriate Dispute Resolution in Special Education (CADRE)
- (The) Council for Exceptional Children (CEC)
- Department of Education/Office of Special Education and Rehabilitative Services
- Disability is Natural.
- LD Online
- (The) Law Enforcement Awareness Network (LEAN)
- (The) National Association of Parents with Children in Special Education (NAPCSE)
- National Center for Learning Disabilities (NCLD)
- National Institute for Mental Health
- National Center on Secondary Education & Transition (NCSET)
- (The) National Consortium on Leadership and Disability for Youth (NCLD-Youth)
- National Indian Parent Information Center (NIPIC)
- (The) National Organization for Rare Disorders (NORD)
- National Scholarship Providers Association (NSPA)
- National Technical Assistance Center on Transition

(NTACT)

- Office of Disability Employment Policy (U.S. Department of Labor) (ODEP)
- Office of Special Education Programs (OSEP)
- Parent Advocacy Coalition for Educational Rights Center (PACER)
- PACER Center's Kids Against Bullying
- PACER Center's National Parent Center on Transition & Employment
- Parents Helping Parents (PHP)
- Social Security and Disability Resource Center
- Wrightslaw

SECTION 504 LEGAL CASES

In addition to the advocacy groups, prevalent court cases have ruled around Section 504. Here are six Section 504 cases that you may want to familiarize yourself with; some of these occurred in work settings instead of schools; nonetheless, the context of the case is informative and thought-provoking:

- Brown v. Board of Education of Topeka, Kansas, 347 U.S. 483 (1954) Least Restrictive Environment/Equal Education Rights
- Sutton v. United Air Lines, Inc. Interpretation of Substantial Limitation,
- Murphy v. United Parcel Service, Inc. Interpretation of Substantial Limitation
- D.F. v Leon Co. Sch. Bd. 62 IDELR (N.D. Fla. 2014)
- Beam v. Western Way Sch. District., 67 IDELR 88, 165

F. Supp.3d 200 (M.D. Pa. 2016)

- Fry v. Napoleon Comm. Sch. District (No. 15-497) (2017) FAPE and Americans with Disabilities Amendment Act
- Endrew F. v. Douglas County School District RE-1 (No. 15-827) (2017) Education Standards and FAPE

There are more than seven cases; one is not more or less important than the other. The above cases are the more famous cases in Section 504 or cases that have challenged or redefined a Free and Appropriate Public Education.

The purpose of the history and case law information is to show the evolution and road to justice for parents and students with disabilities. The goal was also to show that Section 504 rights and cases cultivated historical change. What did you learn, and how will the historical knowledge impact you as a Section 504 Coordinator? What underlying factors could negatively impact your building's 504 students regarding the school culture, inclusion, and equity for students with disabilities?

What will you do to change the school culture in your building positively? If you are not a defined school leader, what leader will you seek to support your coordinator role to ensure teachers follow Section 504 laws and the school building remains compliant?

I am hopeful that the historical background and case law insight provide knowledge, encourage empathy and appreciation for the task ahead of you, and help you recognize the discrimination that Section 504 and students with disabilities have faced due to being "different." The culture has changed; however, there is always room for improvement. How will you advocate for the students and teachers you serve and ensure a culture of inclusion "free from barriers?"

As the Section 504 Coordinator, you must press on and lead the charge for continued growth and meaningful educational experiences for your students.

Here are some **Essential Tips** for leading and changing the Section 504 narrative as a Section 504 Coordinator:

1. Research and review the Brown and Endrew case or any of the cases. Review a summary.

2. Obtain and review a copy of your district's parent rights, Section 504 procedures, and procedural safeguards.

3. Review the three sites listed and gather some information that is meaningful to you. Use the information to make small changes in your building:

- National Center for Learning Disabilities (NCLD)
- Office of Special Education Programs (OSEP)
- Department of Education/Office of Special Education and Rehabilitative Services

"At any given moment, public opinion is a chaos of superstition, misinformation, and prejudice." Gore Vidal

CHAPTER 3
KNOW YOUR STUFF: KNOWLEDGE IS POWER

"You must learn the rules of the game. And then you must play better than anyone else." Unknown

We have all heard "Knowledge is Power." That quote is meaningful in life. We have had a history lesson. Now, it is time to delve deeper into Section 504. We acquire knowledge; as humans, we constantly learn new things and evolve. In education, we continually learn, balance work, and manage with limited Section 504 training.

Based on my experiences, most local school Section 504 coordinators receive one or two Section 504 professional trainings at the beginning of the year while overwhelmed with a thousand other tasks. You are trained in 504 while juggling every other start-of-school-year responsibility. Once the training ends, you enter the Section 504 world to lead and train others confidently.

As a district Section 504 leader, I am provided limited days and time to train Section 504 coordinators. Anything more than a few hours garners complaints about educators being excessively absent from the school building, so I must prepare and train strategically. We often encounter an unfortunate reality in education as educators and leaders—working with limited time and resources to make the impossible possible. School districts must do better by allowing time and multiple exposures to such legal and meaningful subjects.

In many schools, novice administrators, lead teachers, or counselors are assigned Section 504 as their primary responsibilities. Research suggests that most educators lack the course work and field experience needed to lead local efforts to create learning environments that emphasize academic success for students with disabilities" (DiPaola & Tschannen-Moran, 2003, p.11; Katsiyannis et al., 1996; Parker & Day, 1997).

Section 504 Coordinators must be intentional and seize opportunities to better themselves professionally and learn specifics relating to Section 504. Learning Section 504 and serving as a coordinator requires effort. Practicing and learning about Section 504 helps you become a knowledgeable coordinator. Deliberately take some time, such as five or ten minutes, to learn about Section 504.

Browse the federal department of education website and the Office of Civil Rights about Section 504. The state department of education and district sites also have information and guidance about Section 504. Glance through these site newsletters and stay current. Go into your district's Section 504 document portal and review the plans. Read through some of the plans and accommodations. Take hold of knowledge through teachable moments. Seize opportunities where you learn from colleagues who have served as Section 504 coordinators. After a Section 504 meeting, take some time to debrief afterward to learn and gather feedback. The goal is to find the time to create teachable moments to increase your Section 504 knowledge. Knowledge is Power!

DISTRICT KNOWLEDGE IS POWER

In the previous chapters, I mentioned the impact of district relationships with district personnel and the resources your school district will offer. I want to reiterate that those district policies will serve as your blueprint for acquiring knowledge about Section 504. DiPaola & Walther-Thomas, 2003 discussed the need for influential leaders to develop a working knowledge about disabilities and behavioral challenges that impact learning when various conditions present. The authors stress the need for leaders to have a thorough understanding of the laws that protect the educational rights of students with disabilities. As the Section 504 Coordinator, you are in a leadership role for your building. Without a solid understanding of Section 504 rules and mandates, Section 504 coordinators will lack the basic foundations to lead Section 504 successfully.

All districts have a Section 504 manual or place where coordinators can locate information and resources. This manual will have district policies closely aligned with the state rules and regulations for Section 504. The manual may have procedures and guidelines. Create a Section 504 folder and save this manual and those resources for easy access.

Building leaders are responsible for communicating with families and teachers about educational services, promoting disability awareness, monitoring and evaluating educational decisions and services, and ensuring legal compliance (CEC, 1997, 2001; Pankake & Fullwood, 1999). Use those federal, state, and district resources when you need guidance and seek answers with a familiar contact person, such as your district Section 504

Coordinator, to provide support and guidance so that you remain current and knowledgeable about Section 504.

SECTION 504 BASICS

Section 504 plans are plans written for students with a medical impairment. These impairments may be physical or mental. Section 504 originates from Section 504 of the Rehabilitation Act of 1973/Public law 93-112. If you recall, I discussed Section 504 laws in Chapter Two. The Section 504 Rehabilitation Act is a comprehensive law that addresses disabled persons' rights and applies to all federal financial assistance agencies. Section 504 aims to eliminate barriers to education programs and services, increase building accessibility, and establish equitable employment practices. These laws are thoroughly and specifically addressed in the Section 504 regulations (US Department of Education, 2020).

IMPAIRMENTS

Individuals who meet Section 504 eligibility are qualified individuals with a disability and a documented mental or physical impairment that substantially limits one or more major life activities. According to the Americans with Disabilities Amendment Act, "The Section 504 regulatory provision at 34 C.F.R. 104.3(j)(2)(i) defines a physical or mental impairment as any physiological disorder or condition, cosmetic disfigurement, or anatomical loss affecting one or more of the following body systems: neurological; musculoskeletal; special sense organs; respiratory, including speech organs; cardiovascular;

reproductive; digestive; genito-urinary; hemic and lymphatic; skin; and endocrine; or any mental or psychological disorder, such as mental retardation, organic brain syndrome, emotional or mental illness, and specific learning disabilities. Some common impairments include:

- Anxiety
- Attention Deficit Hyperactivity Disorder and Attention Deficit Disorder
- Asthma
- Dyslexia (if not eligible under IDEA)
- Chronic health conditions
- Diabetes (virtually always)
- Psychological conditions (if not IDEA)
- HIV+ status, AIDS
- Fetal Alcohol Syndrome
- Traumatic brain injury (if not IDEA)

(https://www.ada.gov/pubs/ada.htm, 2021)

Major life activities, as defined in the Section 504 regulations at 34 C.F.R. 104.3(j)(2)(ii), include functions such as caring for oneself, performing manual tasks, walking, seeing, hearing, speaking, breathing, learning, and working. This list is not exhaustive. Other functions can be major life activities for purposes of Section 504. In the Amendments Act (see FAQ 1), Congress provided additional examples of general activities that are major life activities, including eating, sleeping, standing, lifting, bending, reading, concentrating, thinking, and communicating. Congress also provided a non-exhaustive list of examples of "major bodily functions" that are major life activities, such as the immune system's functions, normal cell growth, digestive, bowel, bladder, neurological, brain, respiratory, circulatory, endocrine, and reproductive functions."

Some specific major life activities include:

- caring for oneself
- performing manual tasks
- seeing
- hearing
- eating
- sleeping
- walking
- standing
- lifting

- bending
- speaking
- breathing
- learning
- reading
- concentrating
- thinking
- communicating
- working[9]

(https://www.ada.gov/pubs/ada.htm, 2021)

There are three questions to consider when determining whether a person's impairment substantially limits one or more major life activities:

1. What is the nature and severity of the impairment?
2. How long will it last, or is it expected to last?
3. What is its permanent or long-term impact or expected impact?

(https://www.ada.gov/pubs/ada.htm, 2021)

According to the Amendments Act, episodic or impairments in remission under Section 504 are considered a disability (see FAQ #1). Congress clarified that if such impairments substantially limit a major life activity when active, then a student is entitled to a free appropriate public education under Section 504 (US Department of Education, n.d.).

Local school 504 coordinators should have some basic knowledge of impairments. Throughout the role, you will encounter various impairments that are unique. When you encounter those situations, gather data and seek others, for instance, a school nurse, the district Section 504 contact, or even the parent. The goal is to be aware and learn to lead and facilitate meetings effectively.

TEMPORARY IMPAIRMENTS

Under Section 504, students may temporarily qualify for impairments. Temporary impairments are non-chronic impairments that do not last long and have little or no long-term impact. Some examples include broken limbs, hand injuries, short-term impairments that may occur after surgery, etc.

When determining the need for a 504 Plan, school personnel, like special education, usually meet as a team. The team must consider the impact of the documented mental or physical impairment along with relevant information to determine a "substantial limitation." For example, if a student breaks an arm and that break causes a substantial limitation in performing a school task such as writing, the team may implement a temporary 504 plan for the break duration. Once the student's arm heals, the team may terminate the plan since it is no longer needed.

THE SECTION 504 TEAM

The law is not specific as to the required Section 504 team members. The 504 teams may be titled a Multidisciplinary Committee or whatever terminology commonly adopted by the district. I have heard the terms 504 Committee, 504 Team, or 504 Multi-disciplinary Committee/Team. The words are unimportant, but the team members who participate are essential.

Section 504 Teams may include teachers, parents, counselors, nurses, administrators, and district personnel. Team members who can provide valuable information, discuss the impairment, and assess the student's impairment in the learning environment should be selected to evaluate the student for 504 eligibility (US Department of Education, 2020).

When I have led teams, I always advise having teachers present and collecting input from the teachers before the meeting. For instance, if the student is an elementary-age child with one teacher, I strongly advise that the primary teacher attend. Students in secondary schools have multiple teachers, so I recommend gathering data from those teachers who cannot participate in the meeting. Secondary education teams have a lot of moving parts. So, I recommend that at least two teachers attend and provide input. Those teachers may be the primary content teachers or even those with the lowest grades. I suggest those since they may be more likely to see the deficits and need accommodations.

504 EVALUATION PROCESS ELIGIBILITY

The Section 504 process has three components: the initial eligibility, the eligibility, and the plan. Under Section 504, an evaluation requires evaluation procedures to ensure that students are not misclassified or excessively labeled as having a disability or inaccurately placed based on improper selection, administration, or analysis of evaluation materials ("Protecting Students with Disabilities," n.d.). Your local school district should have a process for evaluating Section 504.

INITIAL OR INFORMED CONSENT MEETING

Before initiating any services that may require a change in placement, school districts must ensure parental consent is received and parents understand their parental rights. Informed consent may happen in various ways according to district guidelines. Some districts may title this a referral meeting, initial 504 meeting, informed consent meeting, or pre-504 meeting.

The purpose is to provide the parent with informed consent before beginning an evaluation. Section 504 requires informed parental consent for initial evaluations. If a parent refuses consent for an initial evaluation and a recipient school district suspects a student has a disability, the IDEA and Section 504 provide that school districts may practice due process hearing procedures to seek to override the parents' denial of consent ("Protecting Students with Disabilities," n.d.).

The Section 504 coordinators will usually conduct the informed consent, initial, or referral meeting with the parent and selected team members. During this meeting, the coordinator will collect data, review the reasons for a 504 evaluation, provide the parent with a copy of the parental rights, and have the parent sign the consent to begin a 504 evaluation. This meeting aims to ensure the parent understands their rights and the process before the evaluation.

Once the informed parent consent meeting has been conducted, and the team has permission or parent consent, the next meeting will be the 504 evaluation. There is no defined period for how long time must pass between the consent meeting and the 504 evaluation. The time must be reasonable and without delay. The goal is to determine and provide adequate services for the student to make progress comparable to peers. As a leader and educator, I know that life can get hectic; however, with students with disabilities and Section 504, we must prioritize students.

THE 504 ELIGIBILITY MEETING

The Office of Civil Rights (OCR) and the US Department of Education (USDOE) affirm that evaluations are required for districts to determine if a student qualifies as disabled under Section 504.

According to OCR and USDOE, "The Section 504 regulatory provision at 34 C.F.R. 104.35(b) requires school districts to individually evaluate a student before classifying the student as having a disability or providing the student with special education." The assessments must be selected and administered by qualified personnel with evaluation materials tailored to evaluate areas of educational need." The evaluation may include the student's aptitude, achievement, or other factors being measured instead of reflecting on the student's disability, except where they are assessed (Protecting Students with Disabilities, n.d.).

The 504 committee determines the amount of information required to evaluate the student. The committee should include persons knowledgeable of the student and review various data to assess placement options. The committee members must decide whether they have enough information to make a knowledgeable decision as to whether the student has a disability.

Section 504 of the regulatory provision at 34 C.F.R. 104.35(c) requires that school districts draw from various sources in the evaluation process to draw accurate conclusions with minimal errors. An impairment alone does not qualify a student. Section 504 of the regulatory provision at 34 C.F.R. 104.35 (c) requires that a group of knowledgeable persons draw upon information from various sources in making this determination.

Various data may be obtained from all sources, and the committee documented those sources and essential factors related to the student's learning. These data sources and characteristics may include aptitude and achievement tests, teacher recommendations, physical condition, social and cultural background, and adaptive behavior. A physician's medical diagnosis or the results of an external independent evaluation may be considered, among other sources, during an evaluation when determining if a student has an impairment that substantially limits a major life activity (Protecting Students with Disabilities, n.d.).

MITIGATING MEASURES

Mitigating measures are items that will lessen the impact of an impairment. Congress does not define the term mitigating measures; however, there is a list of measures that include:

- medical supplies
- equipment or appliances
- low-vision devices (which do not include ordinary eyeglasses or contact lenses)
- prosthetics (including limbs and devices)
- hearing aids and cochlear implants or other implantable hearing devices
- mobility devices
- oxygen therapy equipment and supplies
- use of assistive technology
- reasonable accommodations or auxiliary aids or services
- Individual Health Care Plans

In the Amendments Act (see FAQ 1), however, Congress itemized that the committee must not consider the ameliorative effects of mitigating measures when determining if a student is an individual with a disability. Congress does provide one exception, which is eyeglasses or contact lenses. Glasses or contacts may be considered when determining if an impairment substantially limits a major life activity. "Ordinary eyeglasses or contact lenses" are intended to fully correct visual perception or eliminate deflective error. However, "low-vision devices" (listed above) are devices that magnify, enhance, or otherwise augment a visual image (Protecting Students with Disabilities, n.d.)

The coordinator's role in mitigating measures is to discuss those measures and how those measures impact the student during the meeting. Once the mitigating measures have been identified, the team needs to remove the impact of the mitigating measures and consider the student without those measures or supports. For example, if we remove this medication or health care plan, does the student have a "substantial limitation" to a major life activity? If the answer is yes, then the student may be eligible for services.

The mitigating measures may be excluded when the team determines eligibility; however, the team may consider those mitigating measures and their impact when choosing the need for a plan and accommodations.

INDIVIDUAL HEALTH CARE PLANS (IHCP)

Individual Health Care Plans (IHCPs) may be developed in partnership between the school, parents, pupils, and the relevant healthcare professionals who can advise on a child's case. The goal of an IHCP is to ensure that schools know how to support students with medical issues effectively and provide clarity about what needs to happen, when, and by whom ("What is an Individual Health Care Plan (IHCP)?" 2019).

Students with ongoing medical needs, such as seizures, asthma, or diabetes, may require an IHCP. These plans may be long-term or continuous. Students with continuing health needs should have an individual health care plan (IHCP) reviewed and updated annually or earlier if the child's needs change. Parents are a part of the team and should attend and have input when developing an Individual Health Care Plan. Any relevant health professional should also be involved, such as the school nurse, consulting nurse, or licensed medical provider ("What is an Individual Health Care Plan (IHCP)?" 2019).

The Individual Health Care Plan is different from a Section 504 plan. In contrast, IHCPs only address medical needs, including the medication schedule, what steps to take in a crisis, and a plan to address medical needs.

The Section 504 plan occurs when the medical condition impacts class and academic progress. For instance, a student with diabetes may have their insulin checked in the clinic by the nurse a few times a day. While the student is in the clinic, they may miss instruction, impacting the student's academics. Therefore, a 504 plan may be appropriate for accommodations to cover the missed class time. IHCPs may be addressed during the eligibility and annual 504 meetings. Individual health care plans may be considered a mitigation measure since they support the student.

Educators should not be writing Individual Health Care Plans. Completing an IHCP responsibility should be delegated to the appropriate licensed professional medical provider. As a coordinator or supervisor, I collaborated and built a partnership with the district consulting nurses. Section 504 addresses medical needs, so it seemed logical to collaborate and invite the local or district nurses to attend the meetings or review the medical.

THE 504 PLAN

Once the committee meets and determines eligibility under Section 504, the team will usually determine the need for accommodations. During that meeting, the committee must determine if accommodations and modifications in the general education setting are required to "level the playing field" with other non-disabled peers to ensure a Free and Appropriate Public Education. Section 504 plans are not special education-related, and services are provided in the general education environment.

The committee may consider the mitigating measures, current interventions, and Health Care Plan information when determining what accommodations are required to "level the playing field." The team will use that information and discuss what accommodations are appropriate for that student, considering the "substantial limitation." The accommodations must be reasonable, enabling a student with a disability to receive equal benefits comparable with nondisabled peers.

The accommodations or modifications may be adjusted to provide an equitable system for an individual with a disability based on the proven need. That need can vary. Title II of the Americans with Disabilities Amendment Act requires that public entities (districts) make reasonable modifications in policies, practices, or procedures when the modifications are necessary to avoid discrimination based on a disability unless the public entity (district) can demonstrate that making the modifications would fundamentally alter the nature of the service, program, or activity. For example, the school policy does not allow students to access and use elevators in the building. A student with a disability needs to access the elevator; the team would consider what modifications are appropriate and aligned with the policy to provide that student access.

Another example is peanut or fish allergies. If a student has allergies, the district or parent cannot remove what the USDA provides on the menu. Such an action would federally alter the school lunch and USDA program. The school or class cannot remove the items. However, the school may align specific procedures on fish days or have a designated peanut-free area accessible for that student. Schools and districts cannot alter policies but can consider what accommodations "level the playing field" or provide protections for the student with a disability. When determining accommodations, the goal is not to maximize learning or provide an unfair advantage but to provide what is accessible for FAPE comparable with nondisabled peers (Protecting Students with Disabilities, n.d.).

There are many factors to consider when determining accommodations, such as best teaching practices and implementing general instructional strategies. The team should discuss what the teacher is currently doing to support all students and then consider what is required for that student with a disability to access the curriculum or education setting equitably.

Accommodations may change over time. The goal is to provide those accommodations and adjust them to support them as they grow throughout their education. I have advised teams and coordinators to bring reliable data with examples of the student's work. Some examples include parent input, what accommodations the student uses consistently, and what additional strategies the teachers implement to support the student. The Section 504 plan eligibility and plan determinations are team decisions, and information decided should be based on data related to the impairment and the team's consensus.

Some standard accommodations include:

Physical Arrangement and proximity:

- Preferential seating
- Seat the student away from distracting stimuli
- Seat close to the teacher
- Provide proximity when giving instructions.
- Seat student next to positive role model

Lesson Presentation:

- Provide a written outline or notes.
- Write key points on the board.
- Clarification of directions
- Provide visual aids or graphic organizers
- Repeat directions for understanding

Assignments:

- Give extra time to complete tasks (specify how much time)
- Use self-monitoring devices
- Simplify complex directions
- Reduce homework to show concept mastery
- Provide assignments one at a time
- Reduce visuals clutter
- Chunk assignments

- Do not grade handwriting or allow typewritten assignments
- Break assignments into smaller segments
- Allow word processor/computer
- Allow the student to e-mail in homework

Test-taking:

- Allow extra time for tests (specify time)
- Reduce choices on multiple-choice
- Allow the use of a computer or word processor for writing
- Allow the use of a calculator
- Allow the student to mark on a test or in the booklet
- Chunk items on the test

Organization/Behavior:

- Send home daily/weekly progress reports
- Monitor Agenda book or teachers/parents sign agenda Allows the student to have an extra set of books at home.
- Frequent breaks
- Positive reinforcement
- Develop intervention strategies for transitional periods (change of classes, cafeteria, PE, etc.)

504 CONSIDERATIONS

The final few nuggets of information I would like for coordinators and leaders to consider when making decisions come from the Protecting Students with Disabilities site from the U.S. Department of Education FAQ #21-24. OCR does not endorse a single formula or document that measures a substantial limitation. OCR specifies that each decision is made case-by-case for each student, including various data sources and knowledgeable persons who can make decisions regarding the student. There are no impairments that automatically qualify a student. The impairment must limit a major life activity. Finally, a physician's medical diagnosis may be considered, among other sources, when evaluating a student with an impairment. However, it is not deemed the sole decision-maker.

Teams should consider various data, including medical diagnoses, aptitude and achievement tests, teacher recommendations, physical condition, social and cultural background, and adaptive behavior. The diagnosis in itself does not constitute automatic eligibility. The illness or impairment must cause a substantial limitation. In my profession, I have seen many doctors write prescriptions for Section 504 plans. Section 504 plans are educational committee decisions. The student must require the services to be deemed eligible.

REVIEWING PLANS AND EVALUATIONS

The Office of Civil Rights (OCR) and the US Department of Education (USDOE) require Periodic re-evaluation for students served under Section 504. School districts typically have processes or procedures to address reevaluations and practices. In school systems where I have worked, we reviewed a "variety of data sources" every three years and determined if they continued to require services and protections.

According to OCR and USDOE (See FAQ#28), "evaluations may be conducted following the IDEA regulations, which require re-evaluation at three-year intervals. The periodic evaluation exception occurs when the parent and public agency agree that re-evaluation is unnecessary or more frequently if the conditions warrant a reevaluation. The other exception includes if the child's parent or teacher requests a re-evaluation, but not more than once a year (unless the parent and public agency agree otherwise)" (US Department of Education, 2020). School districts may always use general education intervention strategies to assist students with difficulties in school.

The re-evaluation process also occurs and is required before a significant change of placement for a student served under Section 504 in a school district. OCR constitutes exclusion from the educational program of more than ten school days during a calendar year as a significant change of placement. OCR would also consider transferring a student from one program to another or terminating or significantly reducing a related service, which is a significant change in placement. For instance, if a child receives one service but now will be considered for or changed to other services, a re-evaluation would need to be conducted since they are changing programs.

Below is a flow-chart that highlights an abbreviated version of the process:

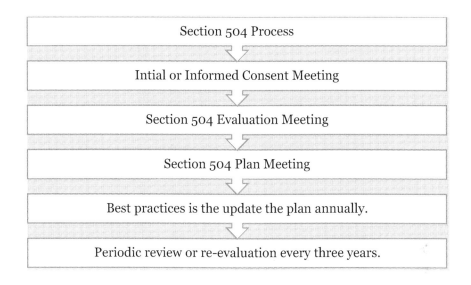

Section 504 Process

Intial or Informed Consent Meeting

Section 504 Evaluation Meeting

Section 504 Plan Meeting

Best practices is the update the plan annually.

Periodic review or re-evaluation every three years.

RELATED SERVICES

Related services include developmental, corrective, and other supportive services, including psychological, counseling, medical diagnostic, and transportation. Some students receiving services under Section 504 may require related services to address learning needs and access the general education curriculum. Some examples include Assistive Technology or transportation. These parts are integral services under Section 504, promoting access and FAPE (US Department of Education, 2020).

Related Services for a student in a 504 plan may include:

• Psychological services.
• Transportation

- Assistive Technology
- Adapted Physical Education
- Occupational and physical therapy.

After the meeting, the coordinator must communicate with the appropriate staff and teachers regarding Section 504 Services. Staff and teachers include the after-school program, cafeteria staff, office staff, school nurses, bus drivers, and other personnel who may interact with the student. All staff employed and covered under the district need to be aware that the student receives Section 504 services, mainly if it is a medical need that may be life-altering, for instance, a student with epilepsy, diabetes, peanut allergies, or severe anxiety.

The coordinator's goal is to provide the information, not invade privacy. The coordinator shares the information on a need-to-know basis since Section 504 addresses medical and disability information. According to the USDOE and OCR (See FAQ #40), "Regular education teachers must implement the provisions of Section 504 plans when those plans govern the teachers' treatment of students for whom they are responsible. If the teachers fail to implement the plans, such failure can cause the school district to be noncompliant with Section 504 (US Department of Education, 2020). I have always stressed that this is not optional and part of the educator's professional duty to adhere to the district, state, and local guidelines for compliance.

SECTION 504 PLANS AND INDIVIDUAL EDUCATION PLANS (IDEA)

Section 504 plans are different from individual education plans (IEPs). Section 504 plans provide accommodations, whereas IEPs address instruction through specific, measurable goals and objectives and specialized instruction. Students under Section 504 receive services in the general education class. Special education students may be in a general education class or small group class and receive support from a special education teacher in the general education class. The Office of Civil Rights monitors section 504, while state departments monitor special education.

KNOWLEDGE OF INDIVIDUAL EDUCATION PLANS

Local school coordinators or leaders need time and opportunities to be aware of special education and services available for students with disabilities. A basic knowledge of related programs benefits the coordinator's role. In education, we have various positions, so balancing and having basic knowledge can be essential when navigating meetings and services.

I always had multiple assignments and tasks when I served at the school and district levels. I was a leader in subjects related to Section 504, Response to Intervention and Child Study, Student Support team, and special education. The focus of this book is to assist with being a successful 504 coordinator. Still, because we often lead in different areas, I will briefly overview some related topics linked to special education and students with disabilities.

The Individual Education Plan (IEP) is the blueprint for how the student will receive services. The IEP is an essential legal document updated annually or as needed. It details a student's current functioning, strengths, weaknesses, and specific educational goals and objectives that measure progress and address learning deficits. Students are usually provided services from ages 3-22 with specialized instruction from a certified trained educator. Classroom and testing accommodations and modifications support the student with accessing the curriculum to provide a Free and Appropriate Public Education (US Department of Education, 2020).

Individual Education Plans are data-driven, with supplementary aids and services providing environmental and instructional support to help students meet learning goals. The goals should be measurable and specific to the student's learning deficits. Once students reach a certain age, the IEP explores post-secondary options through a transition plan. The IEP drives instruction, and the student's special education case manager usually collects the data and monitors implementation. Some IEPs will have related services to address learning needs, such as Assistive Technology or Speech Therapy. These are integral parts of an IEP that promotes specialized learning and FAPE (US Department of Education, 2020).

Related Services for a student with an IEP may include:
- Speech-language and audiology services.
- Interpreting services.
- Psychological services.
- Transportation
- Assistive Technology

- Occupational and physical therapy.
- Recreation, including therapeutic recreation.
- Early identification and evaluation of disabilities in children

The IEP team may range from special education teachers to specialists. The level of related services in the district will vary. Related services usually begin with some evaluation to determine the need for the service. Once those needs are determined, they are included in the IEP to help students attain goals.

The chart shows the primary differences between Section 504 and Special Education:

	Section 504	IDEA
Purpose	Prevention of disability-based discrimination in public schools	Funding assistance for participating States to develop and maintain special education programs for eligible students
Eligibility	(1) Physical or mental impairment, and (2) substantial limitation on one or more major life activities	(1) Student meets eligibility criteria for one or more of 13 specific disability categories, and (2) needs special education services "specially designed instruction."
FAPE Formulation	Meeting the educational needs of eligible students as adequately as the needs of nondisabled students are met.	Provision of an individualized educational program reasonably calculated to enable appropriate progress considering the child's circumstances
Team	The decision-making group must include persons knowledgeable about the child, evaluation data, and placement (service) options.	There is an IEP team with specific required team members with detailed roles, including the parent. There are particular regulations on IEP team procedures.
Plan	Section 504 Eligibility and Plan	Individual Education Plan

Evaluations	Review and consideration from a variety of sources of data.	Assessment-oriented evaluation process (must meet detailed requirements of IDEA regulations) with specified timelines
Programs	504 plans of accommodations, services, related services, and modifications to policies and practices, as needed to provide FAPE	IEP with Special Education services, "specially designed instruction" within the meaning of IDEA, funded through part use of IDEA-B funds and specific services to provide FAPE.
Implementation	General education teachers implement the plan. Section 504 coordinator develops with team input. There is no case manager.	General, special education teachers, related services personnel, etc. Maybe a case manager is responsible for IEP creation and progress.

Source: US Department of Education, 2020

One of my favorite news anchors, Robin Roberts, wrote a book titled "Everyone Has Something," and she was right. Most people have impairments that they conquer every day. We support many impairments with mitigating measures and strategies to cope. For instance, when allergies arise, I take allergy meds, or when my eyes are tired, I wear my glasses. In a perfect world, we use those strategies to level our playing fields and go and conquer the world. Students classified with disabilities also conquer the world; however, they require more support, such as a Section 504 plan or Individual Education Plan, to provide that equitable access.

Here is a visual presentation of impairments:

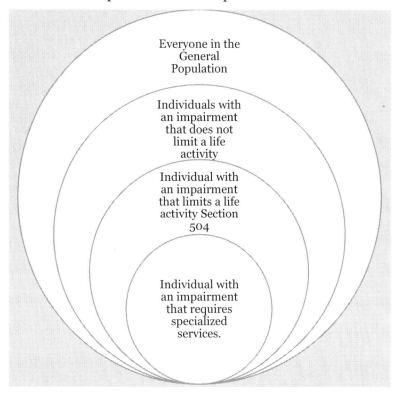

MANIFESTATION DETERMINATION MEETINGS

Students who qualify or are deemed eligible under a
Section 504 plan receive protections against discrimination and
discipline. The team will need to determine if discipline infractions
that cause a "significant change in placement" relate to the
disability. School systems conduct Manifestation Determination
Meetings (MDR) meetings before the tenth day of removal and
removal after those ten days. When I was a coordinator and
school leader, these meetings occurred before instituting short-
term or long-term suspensions over the tenth calendar day of the

school year. The 504 committees would invite the parents, administrators, teachers, parents, and any relevant persons who could speak about the student, the disability, and the discipline infraction.

In 1997, Congress introduced new discipline-related provisions and amended IDEA to address student school removals related to behaviors. Before the amendment, schools removed students with disabilities who had behavioral and emotional difficulties at disproportionate rates. In the case Honig v. Doe, the Court upheld the educational rights of emotionally disabled students who display behavioral issues because of their disability. The ruling stated that schools may not suspend students with disabilities over ten days. The amendments provided procedural safeguards to ensure that students with disabilities are allowed equitable educational opportunities, including manifestation determination reviews, positive behavior interventions and supports, and functional behavioral assessments. The new discipline-related provisions gave school officials the power to remove students without regard to their disabilities for certain dangerous behaviors such as guns, drugs, and assault but also included new provisions designed to ensure that students with disabilities are not suspended over ten days or excluded from school for less dangerous behaviors unless the team meets which is a manifestation determination meeting to discuss the infraction as it relates to the disability.

During this meeting, the team would review current data and interventions and discuss the infraction. After the discussion, the team would determine whether the violation is related to the student's disability based on consensus. If the discipline infraction were related and a manifestation of the student's disability, the student would return to school. During the meeting, the team would update and re-evaluate the Section 504 plan if the violation was unrelated or not a manifestation of the student's disability. The suspension or the discipline recommendation is maintained, and the student's Section 504 plan is updated during that meeting.

School districts have Manifestation Determination Meeting forms to complete these meetings. It is crucial to obtain signatures for this meeting and all meetings. Some districts may not require signatures. However, I have a compliance background. When I think of legal, compliance, and court, the signatures verify attendance and documents who attended and participated in the meeting.

MULTI-TIERED SYSTEM OF SUPPORT & RESPONSE TO INTERVENTION

MTSS is a multi-tiered system of support. RtI and MTSS are interconnected. RtI has tiers to address support levels, whereas MTSS is more comprehensive and may include RtI and social-emotional support. A child participating in RtI receives tiered academic or behavioral support based on data and needs. Response to Intervention and the Multi-Tiered System of Support occur through Intervention Teams.

MTSS is a proactive and preventative framework that integrates data and instruction to maximize student achievement and support students' social, emotional, and behavioral needs from a strengths-based perspective. MTSS is a framework to support struggling students with high-quality instruction and intervention, social and emotional learning, and positive behavioral supports necessary to ensure positive outcomes. MTSS aims to close the achievement gap through early intervention (Essential Components of MTSS | Center on Multi-Tiered Systems of Support. (n.d.).

The MTSS framework consists of four essential components:
- Screening,
- Progress monitoring,
- Multi-level prevention system,
- Data-based decisions

MTSS has core principles:
- Plan
- Implement
- Sustain with Fidelity

RtI is a multi-tiered system approach designed to close the achievement gap through early intervention. According to the National Association of State Directors of Special Education Policy Guide, RtI is the practice of providing high-quality instruction/intervention matched to student needs by analyzing learning rate and level of performance over time to make important educational decisions (NASDSE, 2006). RtI aligns with No Child Left Behind and IDEA 2004, which focuses on quality instruction received by students in the general education setting. Both laws require research-based interventions and effective academic/behavioral programs that improve student performance (NASDSE & CASE, May 2006). RtI provides data to determine specific needs and deficits. RtI pushes a "unified approach" and encourages parent-teacher collaboration in a child's best interest. The RtI team may recommend an evaluation under Section 504 or IDEA based on data collected during RtI or Student Support Team meetings, which may be a position you lead or oversee in your school.

MTSS and RtI can be beneficial when gathering data and determining appropriate accommodations and supports for students with Section 504 services. MTSS is often a gateway that leads to the need for Tier Four or intensive services. The RtI lead maybe someone you work closely with if the RtI outcomes are unsuccessful. The RtI team may recommend an evaluation for special education as a part of the Tier 4 MTSS process. MTSS services may be used simultaneously with Section 504 services to determine appropriate accommodations and plan data. MTSS pushes a "unified approach" and encourages collaboration in a child's best interest.

When I served in various leadership roles, I managed Response to Intervention, Student Support Teams, Section 504, and Special Education Programs. Although these are separate programs within themselves, some leaders categorize them the same, not
realizing that each program is different. The programs may sometimes overlap, as one program may lead to special education or a Section 504 plan, but each systematically supports students and produces unique outcomes.

There are Six Core Principles that guide Response to Intervention:

Frequent data collection on student performance	Early identification of students at risk	Early intervention (K-3)
Multi-tiered model of service delivery	Research-based scientifically validated instruction/interventions	Ongoing progress monitoring - interventions evaluated and modified.

The significant components of RtI include:

Data-based decision making - all decisions made with data	Universal Screenings	Tiered Delivery of Model
	Progress Monitoring	Fidelity of Implementation

The triangle is a general representation of RtI services.

**IDEA or 504
Services
Tier-4**

**5% Tier-3
Intensive
Instruction.
Support 1:1
or small
group**

**15% Tier-2 Targeted
Small Group
Interventions**

**80% Tier-1 Core Class Instruction
for all students by differentiated
instruction**

Implementing MTSS and the Universal Design of Learning approaches provides support and access to learning through engagement, representation, action, and expression for diverse learners, including students with disabilities. Universal Design for Learning (UDL) is an approach to teaching and learning that gives all students equal opportunities for success. Students receiving Section 504 services benefit from UDL because it promotes inclusive and accessible learning environments with varied engagement, flexible learning approaches, supports that level the playing field, and individualized learning opportunities.

The goal of UDL is to use a variety of teaching methods to remove any barriers to learning through multiple means:

- o Engagement
- o Representation
- o Action and
- o Expression

DIFFERENTIATED INSTRUCTION

Tomlinson (2005) defines differentiated instruction as a philosophy of teaching based on the premise that students learn best when their teachers accommodate the differences in their readiness levels, interests, and learning profiles. Differentiating can be performed in various ways, and if teachers are willing to use this philosophy in their classrooms, they opt for a more effective practice that responds to the needs of diverse learners (Tomlinson, 2000a, 2005).

Tomlinson (2000) maintains that differentiation is not just an instructional strategy. Instead, it is an innovative way of thinking about teaching and learning. Differentiating instruction means acknowledging various student backgrounds, readiness levels, languages, interests, and learning profiles (Hall, 2002). Differentiated instruction sees the learning experience as social and collaborative. The responsibility for what happens in the classroom is first to the teacher and the learner (Tomlinson, 2004c) (Subban, 2006). Differentiated instruction and Section 504 accommodations aim to meet the needs of students with disabilities requiring Section 504 plans through ongoing adjustments to instruction and assessment, explicit direct instruction, varied instructional modalities, and individualized accommodations.

When working with students with Section 504 services, it is essential to differentiate instruction through:

- Content
- Process
- Product
- Affect/Environment

MTSS, UDL, and differentiated instruction are essential to meeting learners' current needs and learning styles and encouraging learning environments that support learning. UDL, MTSS, and differentiated instruction are vital to supporting students with Section 504 services, mainly since general education teachers deliver the services in the general education environment. As a Coordinator, collaborate with teachers and leaders to gauge these areas within your building and advocate for developing strategies and professional development to help teachers with Section 504 implementation.

BEHAVIOR SUPPORT & STRATEGIES

Supporting and managing student behavior is essential to Section 504 services, school culture, safety, effectiveness, and instruction. Managing student behavior has always been a concern for teachers and administrators. Teachers report that student behavior is their biggest struggle (Coates, 1989; Elam, Rose, & Gallup, 1996; Merrett & Wheldall, 1993). Both general and special education teachers also report that they lack sufficient training to deal with aggression, defiance, and violence they witness daily (Horner & Diemer, 1992; Merrett & Wheldall, 1993; Ruef, 1997; Sugai & Horner, 1994). Teachers also report seeing an increase in children's behaviors at younger ages ("The Discipline Problem," 1996).

Classroom disruptions have been linked to lower student achievement for students and their classmates (Lannie & McCurdy, 2007). Students with behavior problems are at risk academically and socially. When students find their school experience meaningful, it is likely attributable primarily to solid leadership by administrators, teachers, and peers (Duke, 1987). Students with behavior problems are often suspended, expelled, placed in an alternative setting, and more likely to drop out of school before high school than students not at risk (Wallace, Goodkind, Wallace, & Bachman, 2008). Higher rates of student exclusion from school often lead to disengagement, loss of instructional time, and academic failure. Because challenging behaviors plague inner-city classrooms nationwide, teachers and administrators should develop innovative strategies to minimize negative behaviors. Positive behavior interventions provide an affirmative alternative to punitive interventions that contribute to the school-to-prison pipeline (Losen, 2015).

When I worked as a building leader in the local school, the suspension rates were alarmingly high for students with disabilities who had IEPs or Section 504 services. Students with disabilities often struggle behaviorally, academically, and socially, as some of those behaviors manifest as a part of the disability. In the coordinator role, you may be a leader or counselor; whatever your role, you must collaborate with teachers, parents, and students to reinforce system-wide practices to support behavior. I hope this section will address foundation behavior information and provide resources to support behavior management that aligns with Section 504 services.

POSITIVE BEHAVIOR SUPPORTS

Positive behavioral support (PBS) is a comprehensive, research-based, proactive approach to behavioral support that promotes positive changes for students with challenging behaviors. It involves identifying the purpose of problematic behaviors, teaching appropriate alternative responses that serve the same purpose as the behavior, consistently rewarding positive behaviors, minimizing rewards for behaviors, and minimizing the physiological, environmental, and curricular elements that trigger problematic behaviors.

Implementation of positive behavioral supports for students with Section 504 services offers several benefits such as prevention of behavioral issues, individualized strategies, focus on skill-building, positive school climate, collaboration between school and home, reduction of exclusionary practices, data-driven decision-making, enhanced social and emotional well-being, increased academic engagement, and long-term behavioral improvement. Since many behaviors are characteristics linked to impairments, positive behavior supports and implementing behavior strategies within the 504 plan are essential. For instance, a student with ADHD may display behaviors that disrupt the class and impact learning. PBS provides a framework emphasizing prevention, individualization, skill-building, and creating a positive and inclusive learning environment, contributing to students with Section 504 services' overall well-being and success.

Research suggests that implementing a school-wide discipline plan similar to Positive Behavior Support in Schools (PBSIS) would help administrators, coordinators, teachers, and students employ consistent discipline strategies in classroom and non-instructional areas, such as the cafeteria, playground, and gymnasium. PBS aims to reduce challenging behavior--through multiple methods: changing systems, altering environments, teaching skills, and appreciating positive behavior. PBS seeks to understand the behavior's purpose so that the student can replace old behaviors with new, prosocial behaviors that achieve the same purpose (Carr et al., 1994; Horner et al., 1992).

Implementation of PBS offers three benefits for educators: 1) Suppressing a behavior through punishment is counterproductive and may have short-term effects of behavior reduction (Mayer & Sulzer-Azaroff, 1996; Walker, Colvin, & Ramsey, 1995). 2) Knowing the "why" of behavior gives teachers a more appropriate response to serve long-term interests. 3) PBS works and works well.

Based on research of 109 published studies of individuals with disabilities and severely challenging behavior conducted between 1985 and 1996, Carr and colleagues (1997) documented the success of PBS in reducing the incidence of problematic behaviors. PBS is often a school-wide initiative; however, if it is not, then as a coordinator, I would recommend aligning practices within the 504 coordinator role. `

PBS involves four main steps:
1. Identifying the challenging behavior and why the behavior is occurring (avoidance, etc.),
2. Teaching appropriate alternative responses that serve the same purpose as the challenging behavior,
3. Consistently rewarding positive behaviors and minimizing the rewards for challenging behavior(s),
4. Minimizing the physiological, environmental, and curricular factors that trigger the challenging behavior(s).

Here are five teacher-recommended, proactive PBS strategies that, as a coordinator, you may recommend to teachers:

Strategy 1: Alter the Classroom Environment: Modify classroom environmental conditions that trigger challenging behaviors (clearly define class spaces, alter high-traffic distraction areas to limit distractions, and make necessary room arrangements)— preferential seating as an accommodation in the plan.

Strategy 2: Increase Predictability and Scheduling: Create daily routines and schedules, plan class transitions, and have action plans for planned and unplanned occurrences such as fire drills, assemblies, computer lab trips, library trips, etc.

Align these processes with the routines and procedures and outline an accommodation that supports this in the plan.

Strategy 3: Increase Choicemaking: Give students with challenging behaviors opportunities to make choices. Choice-making should be systematically taught and monitored (Brown & Snell, 1993). By empowering students to make choices, teachers can help lessen students' feelings of powerlessness.

Strategy 4: Make Curriculum Adaptations: Curricular adaptations are modifications to enhance a student's performance in completing activities and reduce the likelihood of challenging behaviors. Ferro, Foster-Johnson, and Dunlap (1996) found a significant relationship between curricular activities and students' positive and negative behaviors. Activities/tasks that (a) students intended to use at home or in the community, (b) reflected students' interests, and (c) were age-appropriate were significantly associated with positive behavior, whereas activities/tasks that did not reflect these characteristics were associated with challenging behaviors.

Consider the nature of the assigned task/activity and presentation methods (visual, auditory, kinesthetic, engaging, lecture, etc.) The interest level: high or low. Pace, difficulty, length, time, and duration, and make adjustments along the way. As a former middle and elementary school teacher, I constantly paced my instruction, took breaks, worked with differentiated groups, and made daily changes. I knew specific lessons would pose challenges, generate a loss of interest, and increase negative behaviors, so I became strategic to reinforce and proactively combat negative behaviors. Chunking assignments, flexible response choices, frequent breaks, and breaking assignments into manageable parts are some 504 accommodations.

Strategy 5: Appreciate Positive Behaviors: Positive reinforcement teaches a person to act in a certain way by rewarding that person for the desired behavior. Provide praise, determine appropriate student rewards, and what the student views as rewards. Use words of encouragement, appreciation, affection, and physical expressions, such as pats, fist-bumps, a point sheet, and smiles for recognition. Providing frequent praise may be a feasible 504 accommodation.

Research suggests instant and frequent rewards for the desired behavior when providing rewards. Over time, offer rewards less as the behavior becomes learned. Alberto and Troutman (1990) have pointed out that the more you reward someone for a task, the less interest the person will have, as rewards are forms of control. The goal is for the behavior or skill to be a reward. Keep rewards interesting and boost students' confidence as students' interests evolve. Remember that the overall goal of providing rewards is to encourage positive behaviors and show confidence in the student's abilities. You recognize their good intentions and believe they can learn and grow.

Strategy 6: Teach Replacement Skills. I mentioned earlier that behavior is a taught skill. Many challenging behaviors occur because the student does not know a more appropriate way to achieve a meaningful outcome. By introducing relevant social skills and alternative responses that serve the same purpose as the challenging behavior, teachers can reduce the incidence of problematic behavior and increase the skill level of their students (Ruef et al., 1998). Work with your teachers or as a 504 team to discuss appropriate replacement skills based on the undesired behavior.

FUNCTIONAL BEHAVIOR ASSESSMENTS

Functional behavioral assessments are efficient processes for understanding problem behavior and the factors contributing to its occurrence and maintenance (Horner, 1994; O'Neill et al., 1997; Repp, 1994; Sugai et al., 2000). Information collected during the FBA is the basis for developing individualized and comprehensive behavior intervention plans (BIPs). The FBA process is a problem-solving strategy consisting of problem identification, information collection and analysis, intervention planning, and monitoring and evaluation. A significant outcome of the FBA process is a summary or hypothesis statement that describes the problem behaviors and the factors believed to be associated with the occurrence and nonoccurrence of the problem behaviors.

The primary purpose of completing an FBA is to enhance Behavior Intervention Plans' effectiveness, efficiency, and relevance (Horner, 1994; O'Neill et al., 1997; Repp, 1994; Sugai et al., 1999). The information collected and summarized during the FBA provides the basis for selecting specific and individualized strategies and support for a student.

The FBA is defined based on four major components:

(a) Identifying the problem behavior,

(b) triggering antecedents or events that predict when the behavior is likely to occur,

(c) increase the likelihood of the behavior happening in the future,

(d) setting possibilities or factors that worsen the problem behavior.

The outcomes from an FBA include:

- A summary statement including the problem behavior, triggering antecedents, consequences, and event settings,
- Data to confirm the accurateness of the summary statement,
- A competing pathways summation,
- Behavior support or intervention plan approaches,
- Ways to implement the plan that specifies what, who, when, and how,
- A proposal to assess the effectiveness and implementation of the Behavior Intervention Plan (Sugai, Lewis-Palmer, & Hagan, 1998).

The FBA specifies strategies and data for teams to monitor the implementation and effectiveness of behavior intervention plans. Districts and schools usually have a process for implementing Functional Behavior Assessments along with district personnel who specialize in behavior strategies. Request and use those resources and personnel when you feel you need support.

BEHAVIOR INTERVENTION PLAN/BEHAVIOR SUPPORT PLAN

A behavior support plan defines how an environment will change to help students reduce problem behaviors, improve prosocial behaviors, and become more successful within the school (Sugai, Horner, et al., 2000). The behavior plan defines what the school will do differently and outlines ways to assess the strategy's effectiveness. Behavior plans provide documentation of professional accountability and consistency for a team.

Behavior supports can be written in Section 504 as accommodations or as an intervention support plan attachment. The goal is to identify the behavior as it manifests through the impairment and identify accommodations and strategies to address the behaviors. Behavior Support Plans (BSPs) for Section 504 students provide targeted strategies and interventions to address unique behavioral needs. The key components include a thorough behavior assessment, clearly defined behaviors, setting clear expectations, identifying triggers and antecedents, teaching replacement behaviors, positive reinforcement, consistency across settings, collaboration with parents, data collection and monitoring, crisis prevention and intervention, training for staff, review and revision, and cultural sensitivity.

Regular communication, fidelity of implementation, and 504 committee feedback are crucial for the plan's success. A group of individuals who know the student well usually develop BSPs—the overall goal is to support the child and foster change in their behavior patterns. The team often will include teachers, administrators, specialists, family members, and (in many cases) the student. The information that is needed to guide the development of BSPs is collected through a functional behavioral assessment (FBA; see Sugai, Horner, & Sprague, 1999; Sugai, Lewis-Palmer, & Hagan, 1998; Sugai, Lewis-Palmer, & Hagan-Burke, 1999–2000/this issue). Together, the FBA and BSP assist the team in (a) demonstrating an understanding of the problem, (b) redesigning the environment, and (c) strategies for success.

SOCIAL-EMOTIONAL LEARNING

Social Emotional Learning is another valuable tool that aligns with behaviors for educators. Social Emotional Learning (SEL) refers to educational and developmental principles and practices to enhance students' emotional intelligence, interpersonal skills, and overall well-being. SEL aims to equip individuals with the knowledge, attitudes, and skills necessary to understand and manage emotions, set and achieve positive goals, establish and maintain healthy relationships, demonstrate empathy and compassion, and make responsible decisions. The critical components of Social Emotional Learning typically include:

- Self-Awareness: Recognizing and understanding one's emotions, strengths, weaknesses, values, and beliefs.
- Self-Management: Developing the ability to effectively regulate emotions, impulses, and behavior.
- Social Awareness: Cultivating empathy and understanding others' emotions, perspectives, and experiences.
- Relationship Skills: The ability to acquire communication, cooperation, conflict resolution, and interpersonal skills for building and maintaining healthy relationships.
- Responsible Decision-Making: Learning to make thoughtful, ethical choices by considering potential consequences (Fundamentals of SEL - CASEL, 2023).

SEL programs are usually implemented in schools, community organizations, and other settings to foster a positive learning environment and support the emotional well-being of participants. SEL programs enhance academic performance, reduce behavior problems, and improve students' mental health and resilience. Educators are essential when integrating SEL into academics and daily interactions. SEL aligns with helping students learn and develop the skills to succeed academically. SEL extends beyond schools and benefits individuals of all ages, as emotional intelligence and social skills are valuable in various personal and professional societal settings (Fundamentals of SEL - CASEL, 2023).

According to research, "the rationale for educating students with disabilities in integrated settings is to ensure their normalized community participation by providing them with systematic instruction in the skills that are essential to their success in the social and environmental contexts in which they will ultimately use these skills (Gartner & Lipsky, 1987, p. 386)." Implementing Social and Emotional Learning (SEL) can benefit students who receive Section 504 services. When you assess, think of the students with disabilities who require Section 504 services and the challenges they may face due to having an impairment. SEL is instrumental in supporting students since it helps regulate emotions, develops social skills, promotes self-awareness and empathy, and equips students with problem-solving skills and resilience. SEL strategies for students with disabilities have also been linked to positive behavior changes, improved academic performance, and a positive school climate. Incorporating SEL aligns with the holistic approach to education, addressing educational needs and the social and emotional aspects of learning.

Effective classroom behavior is essential for a conducive learning environment. As Section 504 Coordinators, we are responsible for fostering and guiding this behavior for all students. Active student engagement, respect for others, and following procedures and processes are essential characteristics of a positive learning environment.

Here are some **Essential Tips**:

- Self-reflect and assess your knowledge of Section 504 services and acquire the necessary training to lead Section 504 services.

- Learn about the students and the disabilities that are in your building and attend professional development to refine your skills and build your efficacy as a coordinator.
- Work with your administration to determine teachers' efficacy with Section 504 services and plans. Plan appropriate professional development to increase Section 504 knowledge, accommodations, strategies, behavior supports, collaboration, and services (Take surveys on staff needs and develop a professional development action plan).
- Identify your students with 504 plans in the building and build relationships, or find a way to track their progress and success with teachers.
- Support teachers by reinforcing skills and behaviors through the 504 or positive support plans.
- Follow all district policies and procedures. (discipline, restraint, emergencies, etc.).
- Seek district support to help with plans and strategies (PBIS coaches, behavior support staff, coaches, etc.)
- Leverage and use any school-wide positive behavior support systems and see what you can offer as a coordinator (chat with the counselor, lunch with the coordinator, etc.)
- Work with your administrators and teachers to establish and provide consistent school-home communication.

KNOWLEDGE IS POWER: ABCS (ACRONYMS)

In education, we use more acronyms than words in the English language. IEP, BIP, MTSS, RtI, etc....are some common acronyms. When I hear these acronyms, I often hum the Jackson 5 Tune ABC as easy as 123! Nonetheless, these acronyms are not as easy as the song and can confuse an already overpowering subject.

During my first year in teaching and leadership, I would sit in meetings, hear acronyms, jot them down, and research the meanings later. I spent most of my first month learning and remembering acronyms. I often thought there needed to be a dictionary for acronyms!! The list continues with IDEA, PSP, FBA, ADAA, and OCR. If I felt clueless as an educator, I could only imagine the confusion parents and general education teachers may encounter. It is almost like a foreign language that requires translation.

Here are some common acronyms and their meanings. There may be other definitions related to Section 504 in your district, state manuals, or website:

504	ABA	ADAAA
Section 504 of the Rehabilitation Act Section 504 originates from Section 504 of the Rehabilitation Act of 1973/Public law 93-112. Section 504 plans are plans written for students with a medical impairment. These impairments may be physical or mental.	Applied Behavior Analysis is a type of therapy that focuses on improving specific behaviors. Examples include social skills, communication, reading, academics, and adaptive learning skills (Psychology Today, n.d.).	Americans with Disabilities Act is a civil rights law that Congress initially passed in 1990 (as the Americans with Disabilities Act-ADA). It protects individuals with disabilities from workplace, school, and other workplace discrimination (National Center for Learning Disabilities, n.d.)
ADHD Attention Deficit Hyperactivity Disorder is a mental impairment. ADHD is categorized based on the strongest symptoms. The categories are (1) predominantly inattentive type, (2) predominantly hyperactive-impulsive type, and (3) combined type (where signs of the first two types are equally present).	AD/AD/ASD-autism disorder Autism Spectrum Disorder (ASD) is characterized by a comprehensive range of conditions characterized by social skills, repetitive behaviors, speech, and nonverbal communication challenges. Autism is a spectrum disorder; each individual with autism has a distinct set of strengths and challenges (Autism Speaks, n.d.).	ADD Attention Deficit Disorder is characterized as difficulty with attentiveness, focus, and task completion without the hyperactivity characteristic (NOLO Press, n.d.).

AT	APE	AYP
Assistive Technology is equipment and systems that enhance learning, working, and daily living for students with disabilities (Assistive Technology Industry Association, n.d.).	Adapted Physical Education is modified physical education. (Adapted Physical Education National Standards - What Is Adapted Physical Education? n.d.).	Adequate Yearly Progress is a student growth measure that aligns with No Child Left Behind.
BCBA	**BIP/BMP**	**CPAD**
Board Certified Behavior Analyst is a professional who provides behavior services.	A behavior Intervention Plan/Behavior Management Plan is a plan that specifically targets and supports behaviors.	Central Processing Auditory Disorder is a processing disorder that makes it difficult for children to process what others are saying, especially the subtle differences between sounds in words (Function Abilities, n.d.).
CFR	**CBA**	**CST**
Code Federal Regulations is the codification of general and federal regulations. In education, these are laws that are aligned with policies in education.	Curriculum-Based Assessment/Measurement is a measure that teachers use to assess primary academic areas.	A Child Study Team, also called a Student Support Team or RtI Team, is a team of educators, school-related personnel, and parents that work together to provide interventions and strategies that support a child's academics and behaviors.

DD	DOE	DHH
Developmentally Delayed is a deficit in basic developmental tasks compared to same-age peers.	Department of Education The state department agency reinforces federal laws at the state level.	Deaf and Hard of Hearing is an impairment where an individual has severe hearing loss with very little or no functional hearing. (DOIT, 2021).
EBD	ESEA	ESY
Emotional Behavior Disorder (EBD) is a specific mental health disorder that causes extreme emotions and behaviors. (Healthy Place, 2019).	The Elementary and Secondary Education Act was signed by Lyndon B. Johnson in 1965. The ESEA enforces a full educational opportunity" for all students (US Department of Education, n.d.).	Extended School Year provides services for students who demonstrate regression over long periods. ESY may be special education and related services provided to a student with a disability.
FAPE	FBA	FERPA
Free Appropriate Public Education is defined in Chapter 2 as services to students with disabilities in the least restrictive environment.	Functional Behavior Analysis is a process for identifying behaviors and planning to address those behaviors.	Family Educational Rights and Privacy Act is a Federal law that protects the privacy of student education records (US Department of Education (ED), n.d.)
GEC	HI	IHCP
General education class is considered the least restrictive environment with non-disabled peers.	Hearing impairment is an impairment in which an individual has severe hearing loss with very little or no functional hearing (DOIT, 2021).	Individual Health Care Plan. IHCPs ensure that schools know how to support students with medical issues ((IHCP" 2019).

IDEA	IEE	IEP
Individuals with Disabilities Education Act revision of PL 94-142 states that disabled children and adults ages 3-21 be educated in the "least restrictive environment" to the maximum extent appropriate (Payne, 2001)	Independent Education Evaluation is an evaluation from a private provider at the district's expense.	Individualized Education Plan utilizes the assessment data to address specialized learning goals and objectives, present levels, educational performance, and specific academic and related services. (Payne, 2001).
IP	**LD**	**LEA**
An intervention plan is a plan that provides strategies to address academic deficits or behaviors.	Learning Disability is an impairment that impacts learning.	The Local Education Agency Operates schools and enforces laws (federal and state), policies, and standards.
LRE	**MDR**	**MOID**
The Least Restrictive Environment in Education is an environment with non-disabled peers.	Manifestation Determination is a meeting for a student to determine if an infraction is related or not related to a child's disability.	Moderately Intellectually is a special education service category where the student has an intellectual disability where the child is slower in conceptual development and social and daily living skills. (Boat, 2015).

MTSS	MID-Mildly Intellectually Disability	NCLB
Multi-Tiered Systems of Support **is** a comprehensive intervention system that may include RtI and social and emotional support.	A special education service category where the student has an intellectual disability. Students who receive MID services are slower in conceptual development and social and daily living skills. (Boat, 2015).	The No Child Left Behind Act of 2001 updates the Elementary and Secondary Education Act, which holds schools accountable for student outcomes.
OCR	OHI	OI
Office for Civil Rights, a component of the U.S. Department of Education, enforces Section 504 of the Rehabilitation Act of 1973, as amended (Section 504), a civil rights statute that prohibits discrimination against persons with disabilities.	Other Health Impaired is a special education service category where a child has limited strength, vitality, or alertness, including heightened attention to environmental stimuli, which results in limited alertness concerning the educational environment. There are various categories in which a student may qualify for OHI (Individuals with Disabilities Education Act, 2017).	Orthopedic Impaired impairment means a severe orthopedic impairment that adversely affects a child's educational performance (Sec. 300.8 (c) (8), 2017).
OEO	OSEP	OSERS
The Office of Equal Opportunity is under the umbrella of the US Department of Education.	The Office of Special Education Programs is under the US Department of Education umbrella.	The Office of Equal Opportunity and Rehabilitation Services, a U.S. Department of Education component, administers the Individuals with Disabilities Education Act (IDEA).

OT	PDD	PID
Occupational Therapy is a branch of health care that helps people of all ages with physical, sensory, or cognitive problems. Occupational Therapy (for Parents) - Nemours Kidshealth, n.d.).	Pervasive Developmental Disorder is a category of developmental delays that may be related to Autism.	A special education service category where the student has an intellectual disability. Intellectual Disability individuals cannot live independently, and they require close supervision and help with self-care activities. They have minimal ability to communicate and often have physical limitations (Boat, 2015)
PL 94-142	PT	RtI
Public Law 94-142 that disabled children and adults ages 3-21 be educated in the "least restrictive environment" to the maximum extent appropriate.	Physical Therapy is a related service where a therapist supports students' physical ability to access their educational environment.	Response to Intervention RtI is a multi-tiered system approach designed to close achievement gaps through early intervention (NASDSE, 2006).
SI-Speech Impaired or LI-Language Impaired

A speech impairment is characterized by difficulty in the articulation of words. Language falls under basic categories relating to communication issues that involve hearing, speech, | SLD

A specific Learning Disability is a disorder in one or more basic psychological processes involved in understanding or using spoken or written language. | SID

Severe and Profound Intellectual Disability is an impairment where a child has severe delays in development and can understand speech but otherwise has limited communication skills (Sattler, 2002) (Boat, 2015). |

language, and fluency (Wik, 2021).		
SP Sensory Processing-is a processing disorder where the brain cannot process sensations accurately and appropriately (Function Abilities, n.d.).	SLP Speech-Language Program or Pathologist-School personnel that provides speech and language services in a school or clinical setting (Occupational Therapy (for Parents) - Nemours Kids Health, n.d.).	SPED Special Education is a service where students receive specialized instruction and an individual education plan to ensure a Free and Appropriate Public Education.
SSI Supplemental Security Income (Related to Social Security) is a federal income supplement program funded by general tax revenues (*Social Security*, n.d.)	SST The student Support Team is a team of teachers, parents, and personnel who meet to develop interventions and support students.	SWD A student with a Disability is a student who has a documented impairment.
TBI Traumatic Brain Injury is a severe injury in the brain caused by various events. TBIs may impact physical and cognitive abilities, speech, concentration, personality, mood changes, or social functioning (Mayo Clinic, 2021).	USDOE United States Department of Education is the federal government agency that creates policy for, oversees, and coordinates most federal assistance to education. (An Overview of the U.S. Department of Education, 2010).	Visual Impairment VI is an impairment where the individual has a significant visual impairment that cannot be corrected fully with glasses, contact lenses, medication, or eye surgery. Blindness is an impairment that a person cannot see (All About Vision Editorial Team, 2021).

Essential Tip: Usually, districts have some reference or resource with acronyms available. Request a copy or view your state department's site to secure a copy of the commonly used acronyms in your area. Saving copies of acronyms will save you time and allow the information to be accessible to use your time researching other topics. Knowledge is Power.

CHAPTER 4
IMPAIRMENTS AND DISABILITIES

"The problem is not the person's disability... The problem is society's view of the person's abilities."
Anonymous

I have been a leader in Section 504 for over ten years. As I previously mentioned, it was a duty I fulfilled and managed with other leadership responsibilities. Still, it was not until Section 504 was one of my primary duties in a large school district that I peeled back the layers and focused intently. When something is your primary responsibility, and your name is solely attached, you tend to pay more attention to the subject. In the role, I became the expert.

When you are the expert, and your job is tied to the responsibility, you become the Alpha, Omega, the knowledge giver, and seeker. I learned to immerse myself in the role, create systems and procedures, and learn about various medical, legal, and Section 504 content. One of those topics that I constantly face includes multiple impairments and disabilities.

"The Education Department (ED) Section 504 regulation defines an "individual with handicaps" as any person who (i) has a physical or mental impairment that substantially limits one or more major life activities, (ii) has a record of such an impairment, or (iii) is regarded as having such an impairment. The regulation further defines a physical or mental impairment as (A) any physiological disorder or condition, cosmetic disfigurement, or anatomical loss affecting one or more of the following body systems: neurological; musculoskeletal; special sense organs;

respiratory, including speech organs; cardiovascular; reproductive; digestive; genitourinary; hemic and lymphatic; skin; and endocrine; or (B) any mental or psychological disorder, such as mental retardation, organic brain syndrome, emotional or mental illness, and specific learning disabilities. The definition does not set forth a list of specific diseases and conditions that constitute physical or mental impairments because of the difficulty of ensuring any list's comprehensiveness" (US Department of Education, n.d.).

504 HIDDEN IMPAIRMENTS

According to the US Department of Education, "hidden disabilities are physical or mental impairments are conditions not readily apparent to others. They include such conditions and diseases as specific learning disabilities, diabetes, epilepsy, and allergies. Hidden disabilities such as low vision, poor hearing, heart disease, or chronic illness may not be obvious. A chronic illness involves a recurring and long-term disability such as diabetes, heart disease, kidney and liver disease, high blood pressure, and ulcers" (US Department of Education, n.d.). With hidden disabilities, schools must be conscious and understand that just because an impairment is not evident does not mean that the impairment does not exist. Teams must follow the process and use a variety of sources of data to make decisions.

The DSM, the Diagnostic and Statistical Manual of Mental Disorders, is an entire of mental impairments. The DSM is a diagnostic tool published by the American Psychiatric Association. The manual is a living manual with revisions every couple of years.

Usually, school psychologists have copies of these manuals. The manual has a plethora of impairments and is a great resource. As mentioned, I have encountered various impairments based on my district-level Section 504 experiences. In this section, I will reference some of the common impairments and disorders so that you will have exposure to various impairments. These impairments have been researched and defined based on the current information listed on the sites referenced. The information provides a brief overview, and as a coordinator, you should use the data provided and your research based on circumstances. As a fellow educator, I advise and recommend that all student impairments be discussed on a case-by-case basis with the proper documentation.

AUTOIMMUNE DISORDERS

Lupus, or Systemic Lupus Erythematosus, is an autoimmune disorder where the body's immune system attacks itself. Lupus ranges in severity and can cause damage to joints, skin, kidneys, blood, the heart, and lungs (NOLO Press, n.d.-b).

Multiple Sclerosis (MS) is a chronic autoimmune disease that affects your central nervous system. Some areas affected include the brain, spinal cord, and optic nerves. MS is progressively worsening and often is debilitating over time (NOLO Press, n.d.-b).

Rheumatoid Arthritis (RA) is an autoimmune disorder that occurs when an individual's immune system attacks the membranes surrounding their joints, causing them to inflame (NOLO Press, n.d.-b).

Juvenile Arthritis, also called pediatric rheumatoid arthritis disease, affects the joints and immune system, similar to Rheumatoid Arthritis (RA) in children under 16. Juvenile Arthritis is not a specific disease but an umbrella term for the inflammatory and rheumatic diseases that develop in kids under 16 (NOLO Press, n.d.-b).

DIGESTIVE DISORDERS

Crohn's disease is an inflammatory bowel disease (IBD) resulting in intestine inflammation. Crohn's impacts the large and small intestines by breaking down the lining that controls the digestive and gastrointestinal tracts. Other areas affected may include the kidneys, skin, and eyes (NOLO Press, n.d.-b).

Chronic Liver Disease is a category of liver diseases that may include cirrhosis, hepatitis C and B, sarcoidosis, autoimmune hepatitis, liver failure, liver cancer, and other liver diseases (NOLO Press, n.d.-b).

Hepatitis: an infectious blood disease that, over time, damages the liver. Hepatitis has two categories, a B and C strand; both may require medication and treatments. Some symptoms include jaundice, itching, joint and abdominal pain, fatigue, and nausea (NOLO Press, n.d.-b).

Irritable Bowel Syndrome is a disorder where signs include alternating periods of diarrhea and constipation. IBS may be debilitating, with symptoms that include abdominal cramping. IBS differs from Crohn's in that it does not cause inflammation.

Ulcerative Colitis is a critical and possibly life-threatening form of inflammatory bowel disease (IBD). The large intestine becomes inflamed, and overtime damage may include symptoms such as difficulties, such as colon rupture, colon cancer, fistulas, and the formation of swellings around the anus (NOLO Press, n.d.-b)

Short Gut Syndrome or short bowel syndrome occurs when the body does not properly absorb and digest food normally because a considerable length of the small intestine is missing or non-functional. Symptoms of short bowel syndrome include diarrhea, fatigue, dehydration, malnutrition, and weight loss (*Short Bowel Syndrome*, n.d.).

Anorexia Nervosa is a physical and mental eating disorder characterized by abnormally low body weight. Individuals with anorexia may display an intense fear of gaining weight. Persons with anorexia nervosa may restrict amounts of food intake. Some characteristics include vomiting after eating, overuse of laxatives, and taking diet aids, diuretics, or enemas to avoid weight gain (*Anorexia Nervosa - Symptoms and Causes*, n.d.).

Bulimia nervosa is an eating and mental disorder where the person secretly binges. Binging is characterized by eating large amounts of food and then purging the food in unhealthy ways, such as self-induced vomiting, taking laxatives, using weight-loss supplements, diuretics, or enemas (*Bulimia Nervosa - Symptoms and Causes*, n.d.).

ENDOCRINE DISORDERS

Diabetes is a disease where the body does not produce enough insulin to process glucose. Two types of diabetes include type 1 and type 2. Some Symptoms include frequent urination, unusual thirst, hunger, extreme fatigue, tingling, or numbness in the hands and feet. Complications from diabetes can be life-threatening if not managed properly (NOLO Press, n.d.-b).

Neuropathy: Peripheral Neuropathy is a nerve disorder with damage to the peripheral nerves. These nerves carry messages to and from the spinal cord and brain from the rest of the body. Some symptoms may include muscle weakness, lack of coordination or balance, numbness, tingling, burning, sensitivity to touch, or pain (NOLO Press, n.d.-b).

Obesity is a condition of being overweight where the body mass index is above the average. Obesity may cause other health conditions such as heart failure, diabetes, hypertension, and limited mobility (NOLO Press, n.d.-b).

GENITO-URINARY DISORDERS

Kidney Failure is a chronic disease where the kidneys are not functioning normally. Kidney Failure is also known as renal failure. If untreated, kidney failure could lead to dialysis, heart failure, stroke, hypertensive crisis, or acute kidney failure (NOLO Press, n.d.).

RESPIRATORY DISORDERS

Asthma is a chronic illness of the respiratory system that involves airway inflammation. Asthma-related irritation causes excessive mucous production within the airways, which results in restricted airways. Symptoms include shortness of breath, wheezing, coughing, and tightness in the chest (NOLO Press, n.d.-b).

Sleep Apnea is a disorder characterized by periods in which a sleeping person cannot move respiratory muscles or maintain airflow through the nose and mouth and temporarily stops breathing. If left untreated, sleep apnea may cause heart attacks, high blood pressure, stroke, and heart disease (NOLO Press, n.d.-b).

MENTAL DISORDERS

Attention Deficit Hyperactivity Disorder (ADHD) is a mental impairment. According to the Centers for Disease Control and Prevention (CDC), there are three different types of ADHD. ADHD is categorized based on the strongest symptoms. The categories are (1) predominantly inattentive type, (2) predominantly hyperactive-impulsive type, and (3) combined type (where signs of the first two types are equally present). Every kind of ADHD affects the brain's functioning related to thinking, concentrating, and planning.

A determination that a student has any ADHD, therefore, is a determination that a student has an impairment to meet one of the prongs of Section 504's definition of disability. The symptoms of ADHD may include significant inattentiveness, impulsivity, and hyperactivity. Detailed ADHD information is usually provided in a comprehensive evaluation report diagnosed by a physician, psychiatrist, or certified, licensed professional. OCR has specific guidance about ADHD (US Department of Education, 2016).

Attention Deficit Disorder (ADD) is characterized by difficulty with attentiveness, focus, and task completion without the hyperactivity characteristic (NOLO Press, n.d.). I have heard the terms ADHD and ADD used simultaneously to mean the same thing. As a Section 504 Coordinator, be aware that those terms may be used separately or together and clarify which word is acceptable with a school psychologist according to the DSM Manual to stay current.

Anxiety Disorder is a mental disorder where the person consistently experiences fear, worry, or phobias impacting daily living. Anxiety falls under various categories, such as generalized anxiety, panic disorders, phobias, and selected mutism. (Usually, with anxiety diagnosis, the physician will specify the symptoms based on the individual evaluation) (*NIMH » Anxiety Disorders*, n.d.).

Generalized Anxiety Disorder is characterized by excessive anxiety or worries about various things such as personal health, work, social interactions, and everyday routine life circumstances. Fear and anxiety can cause significant problems in areas of a person's life (*NIMH » Anxiety Disorders*, n.d.).

Panic disorder is a disorder where the individual has recurrent unexpected panic attacks. Panic attacks are sudden periods of intense fear that come on quickly and reach their peak within minutes (*NIMH » Anxiety Disorders*, n.d.).

A phobia is a disorder where the person has a tense fear of—or aversion to—specific objects or situations (*NIMH » Anxiety Disorders*, n.d.).

Social anxiety disorder is a condition where the individual has an intense fear of, or anxiety toward, social or performance situations (*NIMH » Anxiety Disorders*, n.d.).

Separation Anxiety disorder is an anxiety disorder where individuals fear being apart from people to whom they are attached (*NIMH » Anxiety Disorders*, n.d.).

Selective Mutism is an anxiety disorder when the individual fails to speak in specific social situations despite having average language skills (*NIMH » Anxiety Disorders*, n.d.).

Autism Spectrum Disorders (ASD) is characterized by a comprehensive range of conditions characterized by challenges with social skills, repetitive behaviors, speech, and nonverbal communication. Autism is a spectrum disorder; each individual with autism has a distinct set of strengths and challenges (Autism Speaks, n.d.).

Asperger's Disorder is categorized under the Autism Disorder umbrella. This change occurred in 2013, so any Asperger's information would be located under Autism (Autism Speaks, n.d.).

Bipolar Disorder is a mental disorder that causes unusual shifts in mood, energy, activity levels, concentration, and the ability to carry out daily tasks. Symptoms may include periods of abnormally intense emotions, changes in sleep patterns and activity levels, and uncharacteristic behaviors. There are three types of Bipolar Disorders. They are named Bipolar 1, Bipolar 2, and Cyclothymic disorder (National Institute for Mental Health, n.d.).

Depression, or major depressive disorder, is a mood disorder that affects how individuals think, feel, and manage daily activities. Depression may impact sleeping, eating, or working. Depression has many forms, such as bipolar depression, post-partum depression, persistent depressive disorder, and psychotic depressive disorder. Some symptoms of depression include irritability, mood changes, lack of sleep, sadness, and lack of energy. Individuals with depression will have specific symptoms diagnosed by a medical professional (National Institute for Mental Health, n.d.).

PTSD, Post Traumatic Stress Disorder, is a disorder that happens after seeing or going through a traumatic event involving injury. PTSD is a symptom that may be specific to the individual; however, some common symptoms are avoidance, emotional or physical distress, lack of interest, nightmares, lack of eating or sleeping, etc. (Mayo Clinic, 2018).

Schizophrenia is a severe mental illness that affects how a person thinks, feels, and behaves. Symptoms include psychosis, altered perception, abnormal thinking, odd behaviors, hallucinations, and delusions. If left untreated, schizophrenia can be disabling (National Institute for Mental Health, n.d.).

LEARNING DISABILITIES

Dyslexia is a specific learning disability that involves difficulties in reading due to problems identifying speech sounds and learning how they relate to letters and words (decoding). Dyslexia affects areas of the brain that process language. Symptoms of dyslexia include letter reversals, difficulties with reading or spelling, and other deficits with spelling, reading, and writing. Dyslexia is usually diagnosed by a licensed clinical professional or a school evaluation (Mayo Clinic, 2017).

Dyscalculia is a math learning disability that impairs the ability to solve mathematical problems. Some symptoms include losing count, math anxiety, lacking basic number sense, etc. Dyscalculia is usually diagnosed by a licensed professional based on an evaluation measuring four math categories: Computational skills, mental computation, qualitative reasoning, and math fluency (WebMD, 2016).

Dysgraphia is a neurological disorder characterized by writing disabilities. Dysgraphia is an impairment in written expression. Symptoms of dysgraphia include unclear, fluctuating, or erratic handwriting, often with different slants, shapes, upper- and lower-case letters, and cursive and print styles. Dysgraphia is usually diagnosed by a licensed professional based on an evaluation (WebMD, 2016).

Emotional/Behavioral Disorder (EBD) is a specific mental health disorder that causes extreme difficulties with emotions and behaviors. Emotional and behavioral disorder (EBD) makes it difficult for individuals to regulate emotions and make appropriate behavior choices in a wide variety of situations. Some characteristics of EBD may include impulsiveness, short attention span, physical aggression, such as acting out or fighting, defiance, and refusal to follow the rules. EBD characteristics differ for individuals diagnosed by a licensed medical or clinical provider through school evaluations (Healthy Place, 2019).

A disruption in the processing and organization of sensory information characterizes Processing Disorders. Some types of processing disorders include auditory processing, visual processing, and sensory processing disorders. The brain has difficulty receiving and responding to materials that come through the senses.

Auditory processing is a disorder that makes it difficult for children to process what others are saying, especially the subtle differences between sounds in words.

Visual processing is a condition that makes it challenging to interpret visual information.

Sensory processing is a processing disorder where the brain cannot process sensations accurately and appropriately (Function Abilities, n.d.).

Specific Learning Disability (SLD) is a disorder in one or more basic psychological processes involved in understanding or using spoken or written language. SLD may reveal itself in an imperfect ability to listen, think, read, write, spell, or perform mathematical calculations. Symptoms are different based on the individual. Some common symptoms include difficulties with oral expression, listening comprehension, written expression, basic reading skills, math reasoning, and comprehension.

SLD is typically diagnosed by a licensed medical or clinical provider and through school evaluations (Project Ideal, n.d.).

MUSCULOSKELETAL IMPAIRMENTS - BONE, JOINT & TISSUE DISORDERS

Degenerative Disc Disease is a back disorder with a bulging disc or herniated disc due to pressure upon an intervertebral disc that results in a protrusion from the disc (NOLO Press, n.d.-b). DDD may cause problems with sitting, standing, and other mobility tasks.

Carpal Tunnel Syndrome occurs when pressure on a nerve in the wrist is caused by swelling. Symptoms of carpal tunnel syndrome include weakness in the hand, numbness or tingling in the hands, difficulty moving your fingers, difficulty gripping or carrying items, and pain in the arm, wrist, and writing (NOLO Press, n.d.-b).

Scoliosis is a condition where an abnormal curve in the spine can cause your spine to have a "C" or "S" shape. Difficulties from scoliosis can include mobility problems, breathing problems, persistent back pain, and spine or nerve damage (NOLO Press, n.d.-b).

Fibromyalgia is a disorder characterized by widespread musculoskeletal pain, fatigue, sleep, memory, and mood issues. Symptoms often begin after an event, such as physical trauma, surgery, infection, or significant psychological stress. Symptoms include headaches, temporomandibular joint (TMJ) disorders, irritable bowel syndrome, anxiety, and depression. Women are more likely to develop fibromyalgia than men (Mayo Clinic, 2020).

CANCER

Cancer is a severe life-threatening disorder that affects the normal cells in the body, and when old or abnormal cells do not die when they should. There are two categories of cancer. The first type of cancer is hematologic cancers, known as cancers of the blood cells, including leukemia, lymphoma, and multiple myeloma. The other type is solid tumor cancers that impact other body organs or tissues. The most common solid tumors are breast, prostate, lung, and colorectal cancers. Cancer can have many forms, and symptoms may be tailored to the location of the illness and the stages (American Cancer Society, n.d.).

OTHER DISORDERS

Chronic pain is when an individual has constant or persistent pain that is longer than the usual acute illness or injury course or lasts more than three to six months. Areas could include the back, headaches, joint pain, etc. (NOLO Press, n.d.-b).

Chronic Migraines: a disorder where migraine headaches frequently occur more than fifteen or more days within three months and cause severe throbbing head pain or a pulsing sensation, usually on one side of the head. It is often accompanied by nausea, vomiting, and extreme sensitivity to light and sound (Mayo Clinic *Migraine - Symptoms and Causes*, 2020).

Epilepsy is a brain disorder that causes recurring seizures. It can result from a condition such as cerebral palsy or strokes, but there is often no known cause. Symptoms of an episode may range from simple staring spells to convulsions and loss of consciousness (NOLO Press, n.d.-b).

Deaf/Hard of Hearing is an impairment where an individual has a hearing loss so severe that there is very little or no functional hearing. Hard hearing is a hearing loss where there may be enough residual hearing that an auditory device, such as a hearing aid or FM system, provides adequate assistance to process speech (DOIT, 2021).

Low Vision/Blindness is an impairment where the individual has a significant visual impairment that cannot be corrected fully with glasses, contact lenses, medication, or eye surgery. Blindness is an impairment that a person cannot see (All About Vision Editorial Team, 2021).

Narcolepsy is a chronic sleep disorder characterized by intense daytime drowsiness and sudden attacks of sleep. Symptoms may include extreme drowsiness, sleep paralysis, hallucinations, sudden loss of muscle tone, and rapid eye movement changes (Mayo Clinic, 2020b).

A concussion is a traumatic brain injury that affects your brain function. Effects are usually temporary but can include headaches and concentration, memory, balance, and coordination problems. Symptoms may include headaches, memory loss (amnesia), confusion, nausea, and blurry vision (Mayo Clinic, 2020a).

Sickle cell anemia is an inherited red blood cell disorder in which there are not enough healthy red blood cells to carry oxygen throughout your body. There is no cure for sickle cell (Mayo Clinic, 2021)

Traumatic Brain Injury (TBI) is a severe injury suffered by the brain caused by various events. TBIs may impact physical and cognitive abilities, speech, concentration, personality, mood changes, or social functioning (Mayo Clinic, 2021).

The disability information provided is a synopsis. I am a doctor, but my doctorate is in education; therefore, I cannot diagnose medical issues. I took the time to research basic information about the common impairments I encountered as a Section 504 Leader.

This section is a quick resource and should never be used to diagnose a student. Disabilities and the DSM manual are updated, and over time, science may uncover new impairments since the completion of this book. As a local school coordinator or 504 leader, you may experience additional disabilities to research and ask your school-based medical professionals.

Always ask the properly licensed personnel when in doubt or if you have questions. Those people may ask the family, the school nurse, or the medical prescriber for more information with informed parental consent. We are educators, not physicians, so honor your educator duty and leave the doctors' diagnosis.

"Once we accept our limits, we go beyond them."
~Anonymous

CHAPTER 5
LOCAL EDUCATION AGENCY-LEA

"An investment in knowledge pays the best interest" ~ Benjamin Franklin.

The Local Education Agency (LEA) is defined under the Elementary Secondary Education Act as "a public board of education or other public authority legally constituted within a State for either administrative control or direction of, or to perform a service function for, public elementary or secondary schools in a city, county, township, school district, or other political subdivision of a State" ("US Department of Education," 2020).

The Local Education Agencies operate schools and enforce laws (federal and state), policies, and standards. LEAs also develop and implement local educational policies and curricula, hire and manage teaching staff, and provide funding to local schools, which usually constitute the school district. Under Section 504, the LEA is responsible for complying with IDEA and the Office of Civil Rights rules and regulations at the local level.

Generally, the local school districts serve as the LEA and are responsible for locating, evaluating, and identifying eligible children with disabilities in their district. Once a student is eligible for services under Section 504, the LEA's role is to certify that the Section 504 team complies with the procedures according to Section 504 and ensures that the student receives a Free Appropriate Public Education (Eggert et al., 2012).

SECTION 504 RELATED AGENCIES

UNITED STATES DEPARTMENT OF EDUCATION

The United States Department of Education is the federal government agency that creates policy for, oversees, and coordinates most federal assistance to education. It assists the president in executing his education policies for the nation and implementing Congress laws (An Overview of the U.S. Department of Education, 2010).

In 1979, the USDOE started with seven purposes, which include:

1. To strengthen the Federal commitment to ensuring access to equal educational opportunity for every individual;

2. to supplement and complement the efforts of States, the local school systems and other instrumentalities of the States, the private sector, public and private educational institutions, public and private nonprofit academic research institutions, community-based organizations, parents, and students to improve the quality of education;

3. to encourage the increased involvement of the people, parents, and students in Federal education programs;

4. to promote improvements in the quality and usefulness of education through federally supported research, evaluation, and sharing of information;

5. to improve the coordination of Federal education programs.

6. to improve the management and efficiency of Federal education activities, especially concerning the process, procedures, and administrative structures for the dispersal of Federal funds, as well as the reduction of unnecessary and duplicative burdens and constraints, including unnecessary paperwork, on the recipients of Federal funds; and

7. to increase the accountability of Federal education programs to the President, Congress, and the public. (Section 102, Public Law 96-88)

The US Department of Education engages in four main activities: 1) Establishes policies relating to federal financial aid for education, administers the distribution of those funds, and monitors their use; 2) Collects data and oversees research on America's schools and disseminates this information to Congress, educators, and the general public. 3) Identifies the major issues and problems in education and focuses national attention on them. 4) Enforces federal statutes prohibiting discrimination in programs and activities receiving federal funds and ensures equal access to education for every individual (An Overview of the U.S. Department of Education, 2010).

Various agencies are interrelated and under the umbrella of the US Department of Education. The Office of Civil Rights, Office of Special Education and Rehabilitative Services, Office of Special Education, Federal Student Aid, the Office of Elementary and Secondary Education, and the IDEA Act are a few of the offices included under the structure of the USDOE (ED Staff Organization, n.d.).

OFFICE OF CIVIL RIGHTS

An important responsibility of the Office for Civil Rights (OCR) is to eliminate discrimination based on a disability. OCR receives numerous complaints and inquiries in elementary and secondary education involving Section 504 of the Rehabilitation Act of 1973, as amended, 29 U.S.C. § 794 (Section 504). "OCR enforces Section 504 in programs and activities that receive Federal financial assistance from ED. The federal financial assistance recipients include public school districts, higher education institutions, and other state and local education agencies. The regulations implementing Section 504 in the context of educational institutions appear at 34 C.F.R. Part 104" (Protecting Students with Disabilities, n.d.).

The Office of Civil Rights (OCR), a component of the U.S. Department of Education, enforces Section 504 of the Rehabilitation Act of 1973, as amended (Section 504), a civil rights statute prohibiting discrimination against persons with disabilities. OCR enforces Title II of the Americans with Disabilities Act of 1990, which prohibits discrimination against the full range of state and local government services, programs, and activities (including public schools) regardless of whether they receive any Federal financial assistance (Protecting Students with Disabilities, n.d.).

The Office of Special Education and Rehabilitative Services (OSERS), a U.S. Department of Education component, administers the Individuals with Disabilities Education Act (IDEA). This statute funds special education programs. All state educational agencies are responsible for implementing IDEA and distributing the funds for special education programs.

IDEA is a grant statute that attaches many specific conditions to the recipients of Federal IDEA funds. Section 504 and the ADA are antidiscrimination laws and do not provide any funding. School districts do not receive funding for Section 504. However, failure to implement Section 504 could result in the termination of Federal funds (Protecting Students with Disabilities, n.d.). OCR monitors Section 504 implementation. OCR receives and responds to complaints from parents, students, and advocates and conducts agency-initiated compliance reviews. The Office of Civil Rights delivers and provides technical assistance to school districts, parents, and advocates upon request (Protecting Students with Disabilities, n.d.). OCR provides regulations and publicly issued policy guidance on its website, http://www.ed.gov/policy/rights/guid/ocr/disability.html.

STATE AGENCIES

State agencies for Section 504 promote and communicate federal special education agencies and regulations. These agencies are usually the State Department of Education. Section 504 is not a special education service. However, Section 504 is categorized under Special Education or Support and Services in many districts and state agencies. My idea is that since it is a service for a student with a disability, it naturally falls in that category even though it is a separate program.

State agencies provide information and support to local school districts. State agency-level services include program information, services to enhance student achievement, parent resources, related services information, compliance regulations and provisions, and educational services. Manuals, forms, budget examples, past presentations, assessment data, webinars, and state reports are all on these sites. School districts usually reference and have close relationships with these agencies for direction.

Many school-level Section 504 coordinators may not directly communicate with state agencies; however, a general suggestion would be to review Section 504 Services or download the Section 504 Handbook under your state agency's website. Become familiar with key players in the state agencies and the resources and documents. These resources will be remarkably similar to your district's data since districts often use the state agency information as an outline. As a leader and coordinator, be mindful that those resources are available.

DISTRICT AGENCIES

School districts have someone designated as the Section 504 coordinator for the district. The district Section 504 coordinator usually serves as the point of contact for the local school coordinators. District Section 504 Coordinators guide and implement Section 504 policies, vision, and goals.

The district-level Section 504 Coordinator provides the same information the state offers; however, district personnel is more attainable. You will work with them at some time as a coordinator. District manuals, forms, documents, related service program information, and parent support are generally available for school-level personnel. The district Section 504 Coordinator typically offers professional development based on state department information.

The district Section 504 Coordinator will be your direct link to the school. Identify your district coordinator, know their locations, and bookmark the information as a favorite. Attend district meetings, ask questions, identify, and network with the district 504 coordinators. Ask to be added to the Section 504 emails and use the district's resources before venturing to other agencies. If what you are looking for or need assistance with is not on the district site, communicate with the coordinator and then seek your knowledge by researching the other agencies listed in this chapter.

The US Department of Education is a one-stop resource for education, IDEA, Section 504, and anything educational. My **Essential Tips** for you as a 504 coordinator are to save the following sites to your favorites:

- US Department of Education: https://www.ed.gov/
- https://sites.ed.gov/idea/?src=search
- Office of Special Education and Rehabilitation Services: https://www2.ed.gov/about/offices/list/osers/index.html
- Protection Students with Disabilities: Protecting Students with Disabilities (ed.gov)
- Office of Civil Rights: https://www.hhs.gov/ocr/index.html

As a District Section 504 Coordinator, these sites serve as valuable resources and are informative. The goal is to share knowledge and empower leaders and coordinators with helpful information. The more you know, the more you will grow.

CHAPTER 6

SECTION 504 DUTIES

"Commitment and dedication to purpose does not require blind faith that you will succeed, only a willingness to exhaust your energy and imagination to avoid failure." – Michael Josephson

The role of a Section 504 coordinator is an essential job. You have the sole or shared responsibility to support your building, ensure compliance, and be the liaison between the school and the district. The role may feel daunting since you will be the school's representative for Section 504. I am not saying this to intimidate anyone currently in the position. The goal is to stress the importance and impact you have leading.

If you recall, I had Section 504 responsibilities with other duties in Chapter One. I took my role seriously; however, it was not until I became the sole Section 504 Coordinator at the district level that I became the expert in the role. While in the district Section 504 role, I have realized that if the school coordinator is not professionally trained or follows district protocols, the outcome can be problematic.

Section 504 is legal, has compliance laws and rules, and is a federally monitored mandate. I have often sat at the table on behalf of the district to resolve or mediate problems due to local coordinators' mistakes or lack of action. My Essential Tip is to take the Section 504 duties and responsibilities seriously. When parents file complaints or others have to intervene, the relationship between the district and parent becomes contingent or escalates to the Office of Civil Rights.

OCR investigations are not fun, and once OCR becomes involved, the district administration and superintendents become aware of the situation. In education, we want to help students. We do not like to be identified as negligent or problematic.

Here are some Essential Tips and general Section Coordinator Responsibilities and Duties:

- Acquires and uses knowledge of Compliance, Section 504 District Policies, and Procedures
- The coordinator facilitates the implementation of the school board-approved Section 504 Policy.

- Develops, continually revises, and ensures the implementation of consistent Section 504 procedures and educational records.

- Develop a systematic school procedure for monitoring compliance with Section 504.

- The Coordinator provides ongoing training and support to school staff regarding Section 504 and implementing the Section 504 procedures.

- Collects and maintains all Section 504 data (504 plans and lists of eligible students) for reference purposes.

- Facilitates Section 504 Child-find provisions for identifying students with disabilities in the building.

- Schedule and facilitate the provision of reasonable accommodations for students with disabilities within Section 504 regulations in the building.

- Schedule, facilitate, and distribute information for Section 504 eligibility, plans, and periodic three-year reviews.

- Facilitate the related services and transportation for students receiving services under Section 504 in the school.

- Provide parents, teachers, staff members, bus drivers, after-school personnel, district-sponsored programs, and necessary persons copies of the student's Section 504 plans.

- Serve as a daily resource to students, parents, district administrators, building-level teams, and community members regarding Section 504 issues.

- Disseminate information about student rights concerning Section 504.

- Schedule and Facilitate Manifestation Determination meetings.

- Serve as the school liaison to the Office of Civil Rights and the district 504 Coordinator. (OCR complaint resolution and corrective action plan implementation).

- Become familiar with resources/information for assistance with Local Education Agency self-evaluation and remediation materials from the Office of Civil Rights.

- Collaborate and act as the liaison regarding Section 504 compliance issues and needs.

- Provide transition and post-secondary information for students before graduation). Ensure graduating seniors have copies of their Section 504 plan and understand how to advocate for the office's post-secondary disabilities.

- Solicit vocational rehabilitation or other services for transition and post-secondary Section 504 students.

- Serve as the Local Agency Representative and offer a Free and Appropriate Public Education for the Section 504 team and district.

SECTION 504 ROLE IN MEETINGS

In a Section 504 meeting, the Section 504 coordinator's responsibility is to serve in the role of the Local Education Agency. The Section 504 Coordinator facilitates and fulfills specific duties. Some of the responsibilities include:

Answering questions related to Section 504 parental rights to ensure compliance
Ensuring the Section 504 process is followed
Responding to and documenting parent concerns relating to Section 504
Speaking on behalf of the district to ensure the student receives FAPE
Intervening when the team cannot reach a consensus
Managing and problem-solving problems during Section 504 Committee Meetings
Reviewing and drafting Section 504 documents
Taking notes and asking questions.
Conducting Preparatory Activity meetings to prepare for difficult meetings.

Participating in difficult meetings is inevitable in the world of Section 504. Contentious meetings can be pretty stressful, so you need to serve as the LEA, support your team, and be equipped to maintain integrity, make data-driven decisions, and offer what is in the child's best interest. Planning, organization, and preparation will be beneficial when difficult meetings occur. Suppose you are a counselor serving as the Section 504 coordinator. In that case, it may be best to invite your school administration and the district personnel to intervene, attend, and help with these meetings. Even though the district is involved, the earnest to facilitate the meeting falls to the local school. In Chapter 10, I provide some Essential Tips for facilitating difficult meetings.

"A man is worked upon by what he works on. He may carve out his circumstances, but his circumstances will carve him out as well." — Frederick Douglass

CHAPTER 7
RELATIONSHIPS

"No road is long with good company."
— Turkish Proverb

The most important characteristic of leadership is building authentic, meaningful relationships. Great leaders possess other factors such as organization, knowledge, influence, charisma, and decisiveness; however, in my opinion, solid relationships top the charts. Relationships take time, but they are so worth it in the end. In my first book, Essential Tips for Special Education Leaders, the longest chapter was about relationships, followed by an extensive chapter on team building. My solid relationships and team-building strengths helped me foster a successful education and leadership journey.

The relationships and camaraderie with Principal Coach, the Rock Star Crew, Ms. D, teachers, administration, and DW shaped my success and made lasting impressions. If I text or call Principal Coach now, he will answer, and the conversation will be positive. As an educator, I can confidently attest that I love and value my relationships with my students. I am still in contact with my former students, who are now grownups and with kids. Yes, they make me feel old, but the lighter side is that we are still connected.

Researchers, theorists, and leadership experts have all stressed the importance of relationships in leadership. Effective school administrators know how to build positive relationships that increase their schools' social capital (Coleman, 1990). I stumbled across this imperative discovery through serious trial and error experiences.

When I started in leadership, I had the ignorant notion that I would bark off my orders and tell people what to do, and they would follow my lead. It was not until I had been in leadership for a couple of years that I discovered literature to support what I learned through the school of "hard knocks," but trust me, they are on to something. I learned the importance of working collaboratively, making connections, asking questions, learning, and caring about my team beyond the building. I grew when the teachers and staff realized that I appreciated and understood how to be a team player versus a jerk with a title. I began to delegate, celebrate, work collaboratively, and trust my teachers; they reciprocated the same behaviors to me as their leader.

While serving as a district 504 coordinator, I have learned that the relationships with local school coordinators impact Section 504 compliance. In this position, I am not the direct supervisor but a supervisor who supports coordinators. My role and position may be perceived as negative and intimidating, but I positively support others and impact change through the value of consistent and authentic relationships.

The influence of relationships is powerful in leadership. As the Section 504 Coordinator, you will need those relationships with your state agency, district staff, administrators, teachers, clerical staff, parents, and, more importantly, with your students.

RELATIONSHIPS WITH STUDENTS

"Tell me, and I forget; show me, and I may remember; involve me, and I understand" — Chinese proverb.

Teaching is an inspiring and rewarding profession. Educators' impact on their students' lives may be one of the single most influential relationships one may ever have. When you work with someone for 180 days, five days a week, it is hard not to have such a tremendous influence. One of the most important relationships as an educator, Coordinator, or school leader is the student relationship for which you provide Section 504 services.

Students with disabilities often have unique and misunderstood challenges because they require more than the average. It is certainly not their fault, but I frequently wonder why some educators see them as more work, treat them as a burden, or consider educating students with disabilities as another duty instead of embracing differences and thinking outside the box. Not all teachers feel like this; however, I have seen this attitude sadly too often as a leader.

Section 504 leaders and coordinators must advocate and build solid and meaningful relationships with students who require services in the building. Students with disabilities must know that you recognize and value their diverse needs. They need to know that it is ok to be different. Many of their school experiences may have been negative, so they need to know that you advocate for them and genuinely care about their success.

Shields states, "Relationships are not merely the beginning, but indeed the foundation of the educative endeavor" (p. 76). She states "that teaching must be based on strong relationships consisting of respect and absolute regard. The local school coordinator must build on that foundation-- encouraging, advocating, and modeling the importance of relationships and positive interactions" (Shields, 2006, p.76).

Students, teachers, staff, and parents must see the Section 504 Coordinator's commitment to the school and the students who require services. Strive to lead by example for all students and develop trusting, valuable relationships with them. Building relationships with students with disabilities is essential and impactful to positively shift teachers' attitudes, perceptions, and school culture.

Relationship building establishes foundations so that when you interact with students and conduct 504 meetings, you can confidently discuss the student's needs. The relationships built will become a constant staple in that child's life that is trusting and lasting.

Twenty-something years ago, I taught first grade during my second year in education. Previously, I had taught sixth-grade alternative education students. I built relationships when I taught sixth grade but had to model a tough, loving persona. I was young, and it was going to be them or me. I chose me, and although we had many power struggles, every day was a new journey. The positive impact resulted in those students demonstrating a year and a half of growth on the state standardized test that year.

In my first few days of teaching first grade, I was met with these eager little faces who loved school. They were cute, busy, and talked all day long. I would teach, and they would play and talk like I was not in the room. Teaching the younger kids was a different experience, and I realized that the tough drill sergeant act did not work with first graders. They were happy, cute, and excited to be in school. They loved school and learning.

The busyness and energy drove me crazy. After coming home, exhausted during the first week, I attempted a different approach. First-graders were extremely different than sixth-grade students. Sixth graders liked music videos and boys or girls. First graders loved Clifford, Sesame Street, being line leader, and reading in a circle on the floor.

I had to dial it back and become gentle because they were emerging babies. I began to build relationships on their level. Children enter school during their first years with so much hope, endless possibilities, and a love of school and learning. I could not expect six-year-olds to sit still all day. I was an educator, not a dream crusher.

Once I changed my approach and accepted that these were not sixth-grade students, I began to teach differently, nurture and hug more, and change my corrective action approach. According to research by Meyer (2000), Teachers can use strategies based on the social interaction theory, such as that of Vygotsky, to create classroom conditions that foster learning by modeling, scaffolding, and helping students to construct understanding, with the eventual goal of becoming independent thinkers and problem solvers (p. 228).

I created procedures and routines with fewer rules, made a tattletale bucket, gave snacks to those who did not have one, provided extra recess and story time, etc. I had order, routines, a designated line leader, and class duties, and I ran my class based on what was valuable to first graders. After the first 90 days, I had built the best relationships with those first graders. By the end of the year, that class was one of the best classes I ever taught, and their standardized test scores soared. They left my class as independent readers and LOVED their teacher. I remember I was absent and had a substitute, and the sub told me they were crying because I was absent.

The point of that story is that every student with or without disabilities enters schools with those same feelings of eagerness, innocence, and energy to grow; however, some educators and the lack of positive relationships change those students over the years and become dream bashers.

In the 1992 study, "Overcoming the Odds: High-Risk Children Birth to Adulthood," Werner and Smith stated, "A caring relationship with a caring adult enables at-risk youth to make life-altering changes" (p.34). When I compare my first-grade class to my sixth-grade alternative education class, I realize that those sixth-grade students had that eagerness, energy to grow, and dreams when they were first graders. However, over time, a relationship with someone in education failed that student, causing them to be labeled "at-risk" five years later.

Relationships and the link to student achievement are often the outcomes of building solid educator-student relationships. A study by Rosenthal and Jacobson (1968) reported that teacher expectations influenced student performance. The authors noted, "When teachers expected that certain children would show greater intellectual development, those children did show greater intellectual development" (p. 85). You are an educator first, then a leader, counselor, or whatever secondary position you possess as a Section 504 coordinator. Use those foundational education skills to build relationships with students served under Section 504.

Toste (2010), a postdoctoral research fellow at Vanderbilt University, provided research that explored teacher-student relationships with students with disabilities. The findings highlighted that the teacher-student relationship with students with disabilities significantly contributed to a student's academic success. Toste also noted that if students with disabilities felt they had a strong collaborative relationship with their teacher, that experience negated many of the students' negative experiences in school (Toste, J. R. Heath, N. L. and Dallaire, L., 2010). Teachers' efforts to improve their relationships with students can significantly influence a child's general school functioning (Rey et al., 2007). It only takes one great educator to impact change positively. Students with optimistic and collaborative teacher-student relationship experiences had specific positive outcomes in school (Cooke, 2011).

Building positive relationships and advocating for students permeates the school culture and increases achievement results based on my experiences. As a teacher and school-level leader, I intentionally found and made time to value and connect with my students. While serving as the school Section 504 coordinator, take some time to build authentic relationships with your Section 504 students in the building.

Here are some **Essential Tips** for building relationships with students:

- Take time to get to know your Section 504 students. Research who they are and stop by or arrange a brief time to connect.

- Seize any opportunity to connect and build relationships. I connected with students anytime the opportunity presented, such as in the hallways, class drop-ins, cafeteria, etc.

- Greet all students with a positive interaction. Let the students know you care. Have a warm, caring presence and smile.

- Learn student's names and address students individually. Find one tidbit of information and build upon that.

- Listen and learn about the students. Ask questions about their weekend sports team. Take the time to connect.

- Allow the students time to become comfortable with you. Build trust.

- Share your experiences that may strengthen the relationship. For instance, tell them about your school experiences while you all are talking about school.

- Be authentic. Kids know when you are insincere or unreliable and will not respect it. They will respect you because they will value the fact that you are authentic and genuine.

- Be the adult and model respect. Even if the student is acting unreasonably or having a bad day, remain the adult.

- Go the extra mile: Show them you are there and care. Do more than the minimum. Allow opportunities for the relationship to strengthen. Allow some bad days, and do not hold grudges.

- Respect all students: You are the adult—model, respect, and what you expect.

"The greatest sign of success for a teacher ... is to be able to say, 'The children are now working as if I did not exist.'" — Maria Montessori

RELATIONSHIPS WITH PARENTS

"Parents need to fill a child's bucket of self-esteem so high that the rest of the world can't poke enough holes to drain it dry"- Alvin Price.

Parents play an essential role in Section 504. In Chapter Two, I mentioned the importance of parent advocacy for students with disabilities. I also noted that parents have rights and are integral members of the Section 504 team. The parents of a student with a disability may seem closely guarded or complex. However, as the coordinator and leader, you must realize that some parents have reasons for their actions.

Parents of students with disabilities love their children. They have to deal with the involuntary circumstance of having a unique and different child from what society perceives as normal. These parents have been dealt a difficult hand in life with a child with a mental or physical impairment. Often, parents of students with disabilities have heard unkind things and had setbacks throughout their child's entire school career. Like any parent, they love their child, want the best, and would love to have normalcy; unfortunately, it is not the hand that life has given them.

Parents of students with disabilities are frequently exasperated, concerned, and fearful over the notion that they did something wrong to cause this to happen to their child. This situation may not be the case for all parents, but it is a common but familiar story based on personal and professional experiences.

In the Essential Tips for Special Education Leaders Book, I discuss my struggles with my son Alex and the grief I faced when he was diagnosed with a disability at a young age. As an educator, I did not want this, and through some serious soul-searching, I accepted it and became an advocate. I learned a lot throughout the journey, and I am my son's biggest advocate and cheerleader. My story with Alex taught me empathy for students with disabilities, and he has inspired me more than he knows.

He is grown up now and is making the honor roll in college. My journey was challenging; nonetheless, our family was blessed because I was an educator, and he had a loving family, great teachers, and a great support system overall. Unfortunately, there are students with impairments more severe than my son's, and everyone's journey may not include a great support system; however, the Section 504 Coordinator can become a support and advocate for parents and students with disabilities.

The relationship that Section 504 coordinators build with parents should be clear and with good intentions. It is imperative to ensure school practices provide parents with 1) Access: the right to inclusion in decision-making processes. 2) Voice: parents feel listened to throughout the process. 3) Ownership: parents agree and contribute to any action plan affecting them or their child (Osher, 1997). Overall, most parents only want the best for their children. They all are different, and like the students, they have a story. Try to keep an open mind and a compassionate heart, and be patient. Hear them out, use common sense, and remain professional.

I reflect on my role as a district Section 504 Coordinator. While serving as a leader and coordinator, I often attended challenging meetings, serving as the mediator between the parent and the district. When I participate in the meetings, I listen objectively to the parents and school to reasonably resolve issues according to Section 504 policy, data, and experts.

One incident was when I attended a contentious 504 meeting where the student had a disability. The school determined that the student was ineligible based on his grades and class placement. The parent had the student privately tested, and after a year of going back and forth with the school, she pulled out the big guns. She emailed the county office and the superintendent. After she emailed the superintendent, the school, the area superintendent, my boss, and my boss's boss, my superiors wanted me to investigate, follow up, and provide a resolution.

After the parent emailed everyone, she then called me. She was agitated and frustrated with the school. Her child was struggling at home but kept it together at school. Even after speaking to me, she was still terribly upset, and after some back-and-forth emails and calls, we had arranged for the school to meet. She emailed my boss, said that I was unfair, accused me of siding with the school, and believed that my presence at the meeting would not resolve the issue after one conversation. I am being targeted, and I had only one chat with the parent; however, she was now using that discussion to report me to my boss. I was miffed because I was guilty by affiliation even though I had not attended one meeting.

On the day of the meeting, I prayed up. When I have trials and difficulties, I turn to my prayer and faith as a Christian to lead, guide, and prepare me. I read Ephesians that day and put on my whole armor of God. Once we arrived at the meeting, the team, parent, student, and grandparent who was a retired educator participated and provided input.

I facilitated the eligibility and plan since there was a lot of tension between the school and the parent. I explained every detail to the parent, addressed the new data provided to the school, discussed the information with our school psychologist, determined the student eligible with team consensus, and provided appropriate accommodations. In the meeting, I assured the student that he was valued and heard and that his education mattered.

The student was visibly upset during the meeting. He felt pushed aside and angry because his mom had fought so hard to get him assistance through costly private testing, and the school did not consider the information or his mother's voice as his advocate. The school and parents differed on some accommodations, so I proposed collecting and revisiting the data using those accommodations. The committee agreed, and we decided to reconvene in four to six weeks.

When the meeting ended, the local school 504 coordinators were unhappy because we found the student eligible. When the committee considered the new information, there was a "substantial limitation" to a major life activity, including learning. The students' scores were elevated in areas that demonstrated a "substantial limitation" with mitigating measures in the evaluation; the elevated scores showed an impairment even with mitigating measures. If we removed the mitigating measures, the impairment would be severe, making the student eligible. The school should have reconvened and considered the new information to determine eligibility based on the parent's information and request. The school's failure to adhere to policies ended the meeting with one angry administrator, an upset high school student, a relieved and exhausted parent, and me, the District Coordinator, caught in the middle of enforcing the district's policy.

After the meeting, the family thanked me, and I got into my car to drive back to the office. While en route, my secretary called and said that the family (who just attended the meeting) had called looking for me. The parent and grandmother wondered if I was still close to the school. Puzzled, I said yes, thinking what now. The parent then asked me if I would return to the school and calm the upset student until they returned. The parent was so impressed with my advocacy for her child she chose me to help until she returned. Talk about a turn of events. The parent and the grandmother said they appreciated my advocacy and commitment to students and wanted me to talk to the students because they trusted me. What an honor.

I went back and talked to that young man and told him he was destined for greatness and that he needed to forgive all the past resentment and move forward. By the time I finished talking to him, his mother and grandmother returned, and his anger ceased to exist.

By the end of the ordeal, we talked, hugged, and became his unit of supporters. After the meeting, the parent emailed the superintendent, assistant superintendent, the school, the area superintendent, my boss, and my boss's boss and told them that I was an outstanding leader who led with integrity and was instrumental in resolving the Section 504 issues to support her child.

The student graduated a year later, and his family and I are still connected. He is doing great and getting the accommodations needed to be successful in college. This incident reveals a Section 504 coordinator's impact and the importance of building relationships with parents. I have created similar relationships where the parents trust me and know that I will act with integrity and fairness and follow the policy using data.

The National Education Association states, "Parent, family, and community involvement in education correlate with higher academic performance and school improvement. Research cites that Parent-family community involvement is crucial in addressing the school drop-out crisis. Strong school-family-community partnerships foster advanced educational aspirations and student motivation. The impact of parental involvement and achievement is evident at all levels, regardless of the parent's education, family income, or background. The research shows that parent involvement affects minority students' academic achievement across all races" (National Education Association, 2008, p.11). A leader who develops strong relationships with parents is more likely to become involved in the school community, which will strongly impact the school's global effectiveness and inclusiveness. The principal will be instrumental in modeling and setting the appropriate positive tone and connections with parents (Stewart, 2011).

Research has shown that parents are considered "experts" about their children and want to do what is best for them (Friend & Cook, 2003; Turnbull & Turnbull, 2001). Focus on building your parental relationships early as a Section 504 Coordinator. Take time to talk to teachers, department chairs, and feeder schools to identify those "high maintenance or litigious" parents. Learn their names and research the history of their child. Review the psychological report, records, discipline history, and previous meeting minutes and notes. Proactively know the student and parents and be prepared.

My positive, strong relationships with parents have garnered me the nickname "The Parent Whisperer" because I could calm down and win over 95% of demanding parents. I continually try to live up to that name. My secret is simple: Listen, Show EMPATHY, Communicate, Be Transparent, Respectful, and Care ABOUT THEIR CHILD. Focus on those things first.

When faced with angry, challenging parents, it helps to ask yourself from the parent's perspective, "If I had a child in school":

1. How and when would I want to be treated?
2. Do I feel like the school is listening? Does my voice matter?
3. Do I feel that this person genuinely cares about my child?

I advise the Section 504 Coordinator to work collaboratively with parents but always document and tread caution. Always be professional, remain ethical, and treat parents respectfully, even when it is difficult. I am not condoning being disrespected or belittled. Try to see things from the parent's perspective. Overall, do what is best for the student regardless of your relationship with the parent. Parent and school relationships should be a "two-way partnership" with a mutual effort toward a shared goal: the student. Overall, parent relationship responsibility should work with the explicit purpose of supporting students as learners. (Christenson & Sheridan, 2001).

Here are some **Essential Tips** and suggestions for working with parents:

- Listen actively.
- Model and demonstrate respect
- Communicate promptly. Try to respond to calls or emails within 48 hours or less.
- Work to remove barriers between parents and teachers. Serve as the liaison, which may require teachers copying you in emails relating to Section 504 or keeping a Section 504 notebook that manages Section 504 parent/teacher communication dates, etc.
- Be responsive but investigate matters before following up. Let the parent know you are investigating and will get back to them.
- Talk to parents, not at them. Watch the acronyms and education talk. Explain the 504 Process and answer questions. If you do not know the process for the answer, find out.
- Allow sometime before you respond if a parent attacks you on the phone or email. Step away, and when you respond, focus on the issue, not feelings. Bullet points are excellent for directly responding. Keep it clear and concise.
- When parents are yelling and confrontational, remain calm and move away from the crowd.
- Document everything: emails, phone calls, visits, etc.
- Communicate with your school administration or principal about challenging circumstances.
- Consistently communicate and follow up multiple

times.
- Support and intervene with parent issues with teachers.
- Be authentic, honest, and relatable. Refrain from getting too personal. Keep conversations student-centered, professional, and cordial.
- Speak to parents outside of school, for example, at school functions, local games, PTO meetings, etc. Speak and move along. This should not serve as conference or complaint time for you or the parent.
- Take the high road and always remain professional and ethical.
- Be SMART and use common sense. This includes social media, personal calls, texts, etc.
- Remain Ethical. Follow the district's special education policy and the state's professional standard commission's code of conduct.

"Children have never been very good at listening to their elders, but they have never failed to imitate them."– James Baldwin

RELATIONSHIPS WITH TEACHERS

Teaching is a stressful but rewarding profession. Educators multitask various duties while educating students. Adding Section 504 responsibilities into the equation could make things overwhelming for teachers. Smith (2002) stated that Section 504 is not the responsibility of special education teachers; more accurately, it is the responsibility of general education. All institutions receiving federal financial assistance must comply with Section 504. Therefore, general education teachers need to understand the educational implications of Section 504 regarding students in their classrooms.

Section 504 Coordinators must ensure teachers feel supported while educating students with disabilities. Research, articles, and journals explore the positive correlation between administrator-teacher relationships and student achievement. Let's face it: teachers are the focal point of any classroom. The leader's role is to improve teacher perceptions by investing in quality relationships, building confidence, and developing trusting relationships that support the district's Section 504 mission. When leaders build solid relationships and remove barriers, the school's academic achievement will be positively impacted (Brookover et al., 1978).

The theories of Rosenthal and Jacobson (1968) support the notion that teacher expectations influence student performance. The theorists explain, "When teachers expected that certain children would show greater intellectual development, those children did show greater intellectual development" (p. 85). Rosenthal and Jacobson's central debate was that teachers' expectations determine their behavior toward students, raising students' performance. Rosenthal and Jacobson's study confirmed that teachers' expectations matter and suggested that teachers can, intentionally or unintentionally, reinforce existing class, ethnic, and gender inequalities. Students with disabilities are not excluded from this phenomenon. Teachers' attitudes towards students influence academic success.

In the Section 504 coordinator role, I learned to 1) Educate teachers about Section 504, 2) Provide ongoing collaboration and communication regarding students and accommodations, and 3) work to find ways to infuse Section 504 into daily teaching. As the Section 504 leader for general education teachers, you must establish meaningful relationships and reasonably advocate for students with disabilities.

The coordinator is the liaison between teachers, parents, and students with disabilities. As the Section 504 expert, you must know Section 504 content and provide support and resources to empower teachers. According to research, "School leaders who clearly understand the needs of students with disabilities, IDEA, and the instructional challenges that educators who work with students with disabilities encounter are better equipped to provide practical support (DiPaola & Walther-Thomas, 2003)".

As a local school leader and Section 504 coordinator, I provided the teachers with copies of Section 504 plans for the students they taught. I also maintained documents on a shared drive. I presented Section 504 content at faculty meetings early in the year and provided accommodation tracking forms. Once I presented, I emailed the teachers periodically to ensure they followed the plans and offered support.

Before the annual meetings, I had the teachers submit an input form that I created to gather data about accommodations utilized in class, grades, and progress. I also tried to do annual meetings early in the year, like September or October. I called these meetings 504-a-thons like a marathon because we met back-to-back every day. The team met earlier in the year and completed 80% of the 504 plans, so I did not have to keep pulling teachers or interrupting instruction throughout the year.

Teachers have many meetings, so I wanted to remove the 504 plan meetings from their schedule unless there was a new student or a need to revisit a plan. The annual 504 a-thons showed the teachers that I valued their time and would only schedule meetings after November if the parent requested or the student needed updates. The teachers recognized that I appreciated their time, and in turn, they were open to working collaboratively to attend and implement Section 504. The support and collaboration created a culture shift for students with disabilities and the Section 504 program.

The teacher Section, 504 leader relationships are essential and can positively or negatively influence change. The stronger the relationships with your teachers, the more you will accomplish as a team. With all the challenges, your role as the Section 504 Coordinator is to develop a culture of inclusiveness. As the coordinator, you can cultivate inclusion with general education teachers.

DiPaola and Walther-Thomas (2003) have concluded that leaders who concentrate on instruction, establish administrative support, and offer high-quality professional development for educators produce greater outcomes for students with disabilities and other at-risk populations (Benz et al., 2000; Gersten et al., 2001; Kearns et al., 1998; Klingner et al., 2001). The shift for inclusion is ever-changing, and as the Section 504 coordinator, your goal is to continue to make those strides while backing teachers who will impact students. A recent study by Gersten and colleagues (2001) found that building-level support from leaders had strong effects on "virtually all critical aspects of teachers' working conditions" (p. 557). The values and supportive actions influence a sense of collegial support and impact school culture (e.g., Billingsley, 1993; Billingsley & Cross, 1991; Brownell & Smith, 1993; Embich, 2001).

Here are some **Essential Tips** on ways to build relationships with teachers based on my experiences:

- Show teachers that you support them through your actions with Section 504 (discipline, meetings, parents, etc.)
- Communicate effectively.
- Listen, Listen, Listen.
- Help teachers understand the Section 504 Process through professional development and ongoing support.
- Provide consistent Section 504 implementation in the building.
- Eliminate barriers that may hinder teacher collaboration efforts. You may have to involve your school leadership to help carve time and opportunities in the school day.
- Provide and allow opportunities to attend professional development and Section 504 Professional Learning Communities with General Education Teachers (They can collaborate and support one another)
- Be an active Section 504 Coordinator (Be visible, speak, listen, and follow up). Serve as the liaison between the parents and teachers.
- Talk things out; open communication is critical.

- Provide examples of district resources and tools for accommodation tracking.
- Acknowledge challenges and problem-solve together.

"A good education can change anyone. A good teacher can change everything." – Unknown.

SCHOOL ADMINISTRATION RELATIONSHIPS

Your school administration's positive collegial relationship will improve your professional practice and be your Section 504 Coordinator pipeline. The administrator's perceptions and support will impact others' teamwork and effectiveness in Section 504 inclusion. If you are a school administrator, this may be an easier task because you are an administrative team member.

Research suggests that the school's nature of administrative relationships influences the school's character, culture, and quality. Positive relationships between the administrators and the Section 504 Coordinator will set the tone and disseminate the remainder of the school's relationships to the students, teachers, parents, and community. If the school leaders feel like Section 504 is unimportant, then the rest of the school culture will have those same perceptions. According to Wheatley (2002), differences do not divide us. It is our perceptions, biases, and judgments about each that do. The Section 504 Coordinator must advocate respectfully for students with disabilities and strategically work with the school administration team.

Section 504 is inclusive and intermingles with many other

school functions. You must know how school relations will affect Section 504 students receiving services in the building. As a Section 504 leader, I always worked and collaborated with other administrators.

Here are some **Essential Tips** for working with administrators as a Section 504 Coordinator:

- Communicate and provide a list of Section 504 students in your building to the school leaders. This will inform the school administration when planning assessments, accommodations, and discipline (manifestation determinations).
- Provide copies of Section 504 plans after annual meetings or house plans in a place for administrators to access.
- Keep your administration team in the loop on Section 504 issues with parents, teachers, or others to support you in the role and ensure compliant practices.
- Lead as the expert in Section 504 and be prepared to answer questions your school administration may have about Section 504.
- Advocate for students with disabilities respectively and facilitate positive changes with the administration team.

"If your actions inspire others to dream more, learn more, do more, and become more, you are a leader." – President John Quincy Adams

RELATIONSHIPS WITH ESSENTIAL SCHOOL MEMBERS

"It is surprising how much you can accomplish if you don't care who gets the credit."--Abraham Lincoln

The school clerk and secretaries may serve as your designated support system. A lot of times, they enter the data into the system that notes Section 504 services. Other school personnel to include in relationship building include the cafeteria staff, paraprofessionals, school nurses, bus drivers, afterschool programs teachers, and custodians. Be a team player with all coworkers in the building. The support staff is essential; treat everyone with respect and be kind. Section 504 is one of those general topics where you may need essential staff support.

When I worked in a school as a coordinator, I often communicated with the school clerk to code the student or the school nurse for their medical expertise. As a school-level Section 504 leader, I had those 504-a-thon meetings I mentioned earlier. When I had those meetings during the designated September-October times, I always invited and worked with the school nurse and counselors. They both were integral members. The nurse provided medical expertise and wrote the Individual Health Care Plans for the student. Her presence was significant because she offered medical knowledge to the educational environment.

My school counselors oversaw their grade-level 504 plans, and I was the leader. We facilitated the meetings together, but since I was the leader, I used that influence to promote Section 504 teacher buy-in. These collaborative relationships supported

Section 504 in the school environment. My secretary helped create my documents in preparation for the meetings. The bus drivers were notified of the Section 504 plans and medical information for students who rode the bus. The cafeteria manager and workers knew Section 504 plans, particularly regarding food allergies. Sometimes, I invited the cafeteria manager to the meetings to discuss parameters for food allergies.

These positive relationships will benefit you personally and promote a thriving school culture. Model and lead with actions as the Section 504 Coordinator. A school is a complex organization with many pieces, from instruction to operation. Meaningful relationships matter.

"There is no exercise better for the heart than reaching down and lifting people up."--John Andres Holmes

STATE AGENCY RELATIONSHIPS

State departments communicate federal information and regulations for students with disabilities. I discussed these agencies and their role in Chapter Five concerning Section 504. School districts usually reference and have close relationships with these agencies for direction.

Section 504 Coordinators may not directly communicate with state agencies; however, a general suggestion would be to review your state agency's website. Take some time to familiarize yourself with key players in the state agencies and the resources available. These resources may be similar to your district's information since districts often use the state agency information as a blueprint. The chances of directly collaborating with state agency personnel are highly unlikely; however, be mindful that they exist.

As a district Section 504 coordinator, the state agencies were on speed dial; however, I never directly communicated at the school level. Retain a copy and periodically review the state's section 504 manual. The State 504 manual can help with compliance, answer questions, and provide a wealth of knowledge.

DISTRICT RELATIONSHIPS

"Teamwork is connected independence."--David Cottrell

The district-level Section 504 department provides the same information the state offers; however, these agencies are more attainable. You will work with them at some time as a coordinator. The district provides resources, manuals, forms, trainings, documents, and parent support. Relationships with these people are imperative as they will be your direct connection to the school. Identify your district Section 504 coordinator in the first few days, know their locations, and bookmark the information as a favorite. Once you begin, email these people immediately to introduce yourself and request to be added to the distribution list. Attend district meetings, ask questions, and identify and network with other local schools' 504 coordinators in your area. Relationships with these administrators are meaningful. They all can serve as resources.

Create a network or system, and save copies of all the documents offered in specific locations on your computer or device for easy access. These resources will serve as your blueprint, and the district Section 504 Coordinators will be your number-one support system. Identify, introduce yourself, build that relationship, solicit their feedback, invite them to meetings for support, and make them a regular part of your leadership network. Surrounding yourself with like-minded district Section 504 professionals following the same vision will be an asset to your role as a 504 Coordinator.

"You can do what I cannot do. I can do what you cannot do. Together, we can do great things." – Mother Teresa

RELATIONSHIPS WITH ALL

"If everyone is moving forward together, then success takes care of itself."- Henry Ford

Solid relationships are foundational in leadership success in addition to knowledge, competence, values, and goal setting. Building relationships promotes trust buy-in and enhances communication with those you encounter as a Section 504 Coordinator. Positive relationships are the substance of what makes a school extraordinary (Rieg, 2007). "By creating and supporting relational networks that facilitate dialogue, support, and sharing between teachers, administrators, students, and families, the social capital grows as stakeholders work together to benefit all learners, including those with disabilities and others at risk. Establishing those relationships and showing people you care goes a long way.

"Personal relationships are the fertile soil from which all advancement, all success, all achievement in real life grows."--Ben Stein

CHAPTER 8
COORDINATE WITH YOUR HEART

"To handle yourself, use your head; to handle others, use your heart." – Eleanor Roosevelt.

Servant leaders lead in non-traditional methods where relationships, compassion, empathy, and traditional leadership methods drive decisions. Head or traditional leadership is a rigid, task-oriented, goal-driven, concrete leadership style that focuses on outcomes instead of employees. Heart leadership focuses more on people, relationships, values, tasks, and empowerment to attain task-oriented results. Throughout my leadership journey, I have learned that people will aspire to do more under leaders who lead with their heart instead of their heads.

Leading with your heart has become a popular welcoming leadership style. Previously, leaders were praised for being rigid, tough decision-makers who focused on results instead of people. When I think of a traditional leadership boss, I think of the movie 9 to 5 with Lily Tomlin, Jane Fonda, and Dolly Parton. The boss, Mr. Hart, is mean and evil. He did not care for others, and his needs came first.

Once the ladies removed him, Lily Tomlin's character Violet, Dolly Parton's character Darlene, and Jane Fonda's character Judy took over the office and innovatively led with their hearts. They had compassion and ran the company where all employees were valued, had flexibility, and could be their best because they knew they had support and leaders who led with their heart.

Forgive me, I am a child of the 80s, and 9-5 is one of my favorite movies. I am making a point with the 9-5 narrative: those ladies led with their hearts. Employee productivity was high under the heart leadership, unlike Mr. Hart's traditional head leadership style, where the employees did not matter.

Keijzer (2019) wrote an article titled "Is it Better to Lead with Your Heart than Your Mind?" The article discusses businesses and the benefits of leading with your heart instead of your mind. He talks about first being empathetic and understanding employees' perspectives. He explains that leading with your heart cultivates a working environment that promotes a leader's goals and values. Keijzer also explains how leading with your heart versus the mind reduces employee turnover and reinforces teams.

The shift to lead or coordinate with your heart versus your head or mind is a process. Section 504 coordinators must be intentional and try to change from the mind to the heart. When I became a district administrator, the first poster I brought from the store read, "Lead with your Heart." When I purchased the sign, I thought it was cute. It had a pink heart, my favorite color, and matched my office decor.

As time progressed in leadership, I realized that there was something meaningful to those words, "Lead with your Heart." Over time, I started reflecting and evaluating interactions and situations in which I supported others at the district and school levels. When I hung up the phone or answered an email, I would ponder, "Did I lead with my heart?"

Lead with your heart as a Section 504 coordinator. Leading with your heart means leading with passion and compassion, making connections, having empathy, and maintaining a human relationship while complying with the organization's mission and goals. When you lead with your heart, you use your heart and mind to lead in an environment that respects and values teachers, parents, and students.

Greenleaf summarizes servant leadership as the administration philosophy, which implies a comprehensive view of the quality of people, work, and community spirit. It requires a spiritual understanding of identity, mission, vision, and environment. A servant leader is a servant responsible for being in the world, contributing to the well-being of people and the community (Greenleaf, 1991).

Servant leaders lead with their hearts. Educators are in the service industry, so it is imperative to coordinate or lead where you serve and have empathy and compassion for teachers, students, parents, and all you encounter. Leading with your heart with the teachers or team means making those people feel valued. It is the heart versus the mind that drives human motivation. Leading from the heart is caring about others enough to care about their fundamental needs. People are motivated by the way they feel and as it pertains to leadership and engagement.

Lead with your heart by putting people first and showing compassion towards others. During my education experience as a district Section 504 coordinator, I always took the time to listen, assess, serve, and lead with my heart.

While leading, I made sure I was objectionably fair, followed policies, and made decisions that were reasonably in the best interest of students. I am consistent with the same notion when I work with administrators, school coordinators, and teachers. I never wanted to be perceived as the "county person" who came from their executive position to dictate and make decisions without valuing and respecting others.

Lead with your heart with the Section 504 team, parents, students, and others. Cultivate a culture so those you lead know they are valued and respected. Little things mean a lot, so do not underestimate an opportunity to show empathy and compassion. Your actions, leading with your heart, and servant leadership may be the actions that make their day and encourage them throughout their journey.

As a district Section 504 Coordinator, I often attend numerous combative meetings with educators and families. I have been in meetings where advocates and parents insult, oppress, and are emotional. These meetings are tedious, draining, and often consuming; however, I lead with my heart by serving, supporting, listening, and remaining professional throughout those meetings. Michelle Obama said it best: "When they go low, we go high."

Go HIGH, lead with your heart, and when you sit at a 504 meeting or any meeting where you are the leader or coordinator, remember that a child's education is at stake in every decision. Behind every emotional parent or teacher, there is a backstory. Try to change the narrative and coordinate with your heart.

Follow the Section 504 state guidelines and district policies. Lead and make decisions based on what is reasonable in that student's best interest. Continue to serve, lead with your heart, and have compassion.

Here are some **Essential Tips** and ways you can demonstrate servant leadership and lead with your heart:

Listen: hear others out whether you agree or not. Listening will provide valuable insight that may help generate the best outcomes. Listening is gathering data.

Demonstrate empathy and compassion: Compassion is having a general concern for others.

Value and respect others: To whom much is given, much is required. If you want to be respected, you must provide admiration and esteem to others and admire their talents and abilities. The value is using those abilities to collaborate positively.

Be self-aware: Evaluate and acknowledge your beliefs, behaviors, and biases. Once you assess yourself, you must ensure your perception or actions do not negatively impact others.

Build others: provide positive feedback and acknowledge their contributions.

Have foresight: think ahead and perceive outcomes. Have a backup plan and be mentally aware by navigating circumstances and consequences.

Conceptualize: think beyond the day-to-day. Be a visionary or a mental chess player.

Use common sense: use a good sense of judgment.

Lead with your heart and serve others. Act professionally but with compassion. People will never forget how you made them feel, intentionally or not; my last Essential Tip is for you to coordinate with your heart consciously.

"Good leaders must first become good servants." — Robert Greenleaf

CHAPTER 9
ETHICAL LEADERSHIP

"Integrity is better than any career." Ralph Waldo Emerson

Ethical leadership is defined by Brown et al. (2005, p. 120) as "the demonstration of appropriate conduct through actions and interpersonal relationships. The appropriate personal actions promote the conduct of followers through two-way communication, reinforcement, and decision-making." Ethical leadership is modeling morally acceptable behavior that is "right" as opposed to "wrong" in each situation (Sims, 1992). Being ethical is about playing fair, thinking about others' well-being, and the consequences of one's actions.

Ethical leadership is essential to educators as a Section 504 Coordinator. Greenfield (1991) notes that school leaders face unique moral demands. He mentions that schools are ethical institutions designed to encourage social norms, and leaders are principled representatives who must often make decisions that favor one moral value over another. Schools are dedicated to fostering the well-being of children. Students have essentially no voice in what happens in schools. For such reasons, the leader's conduct "must be intentional and ethical.

Section 504 epitomizes compliance, laws, ethics, practices, and equitable services. As a leader and coordinator, you must show your teachers, students, parents, administrative staff, and community stakeholders that you act and lead with integrity. Leaders have a special responsibility to exercise authority ethically. Greenfield (1991) expresses that most of a leader's authority is moral and that teachers must be convinced that the leader's point of view reflects the values they support.

Leadership conduct is influential in an organization (Hitt, 1990; Jansen & Von Glinow, 1985). Leaders are responsible for the standards and codes of conduct that guide employees' behavior (Bennis & Nanus, 1985; Cyert, 1990). As a leader or coordinator, always adhere to policies and remain ethical professionally and personally. Unethical behavior is not worth the consequences; such behaviors are always exposed later. Educators and leaders are held to a higher standard. The risk is not worth the outcome.

Gardner (1995) states that great leaders embody the message, advocate, and teach through words and actions. Lead and model yourself with ethical leadership; such actions will impact change, help you remain employed, and keep you off the evening news. Remain the moral compass, lead with integrity, model ethical leadership, and you will sleep at night knowing you acted with honor.

Stockwall and Dennis (2015) provide a decision-making process for educators in special education using a seven-step decision-making framework or set of assumptions to guide the team toward resolving ethical issues. The method highlights steps for special education; however, the process is appropriate for Section 504 and all students with disabilities.

The technique provides a framework that allows the team to filter through the details and nuances that create professional problems in a specific context. The framework authorizes a strategic preprogrammed method that guides educators to think proactively versus reactively. The framework drives the team to examine the context of an ethical dilemma through the lens of four theoretical perspectives: justice, critique, care, and professionalism. Each view signifies a way of seeing a particular problem or dilemma. The framework offers guidance to school teams and educators who may face ethical conditions or issues that may not have even been considered by those who wrote the professional code of ethics for teaching students and families with disabilities (Vergés, 2010).

Here are the seven steps, according to Stockwell and Dennis (2015):

Step 1: Describe the Context of the Situation: identify the situation regarding the student.

Step 2: Describe the Issues Involved: Provide a narrative of the problems and define the barriers or issues.

Step 3: Pose Questions from Each Ethical Perspective That Might Affect Each Issue. Ask questions that navigate the process and remove biases and judgment. Question: Are we stepping outside to find the why?

Step 4: Identify Alternative Decisions for Each Issue: the team reflects on multiple perspectives and generates possible outcomes, solutions, and goals.

Step 5: Identify Consequences for Each Alternative: the team assesses each alternative's risks and possible consequences.

Step 6: Rank and Order Alternatives and Decide Who Will Be Affected by the Decision and Who is Represented in the Process: prioritize: the team has information that can inform collaborative concessions with the key stakeholders affected. The team may also consider multiple considerations and rank according to the best outcomes.

Step 7: Monitor and Modify the Decision When Needed: make decisions and then make changes while monitoring outcomes.

Here are descriptions of the four theoretical perspectives according to the framework:

Justice: ensuring everyone, including the individual or student, is treated fairly and equally.

Critique: view the legal aspect and ensure the laws are fair for the student.

Care: focus on the fundamental relationships for the individuals.

Professionalism: What is in the individual's best interest? Ensuring the education and decisions consist of high-quality education outcomes.

Ethical leadership and decisions are vital to the Section 504 coordinator's role. Coordinators are educators, and as educators, there is a higher standard because children are involved. Children are our most precious gifts, and society wants to ensure that ethical, moral adults are working with families to provide what is in children's best interest.

In conclusion, model and display characteristics of ethical and moral behaviors. Here are some aspects of ethical leadership, according to Zanderer (1992). My **Essential Tips** and recommendations for Section 504 coordinators are to align your leadership with the following behaviors:

Ethical leaders:

Are humble

Concerned for others and what is best

Fulfills commitments

Are honest and transparent

Show respect for others

Takes responsibility

Demonstrates fairness

Encourages, supports, and helps others

Advocates and stands up for what is just, fair, and right

Source: (Zanderer, 1992, pp 12-16)

Now that I have explained ethical leadership, I hope you understand this subject's relevance. Lead and behave ethically and consciously, and make fair, equitable decisions that are in the best interest of students as you guide teams. Remain the moral compass, lead with integrity, model ethical leadership, and you will rest knowing that you have honored your commitment to children and acted with honor.

"Management is doing things right; leadership is doing the right things." Peter F. Drucker

CHAPTER 10
ESSENTIAL TIPS & RECOMMENDATIONS

"If your actions inspire others to dream more, learn more, do more, and become more, you are a leader."
John Quincy Adams

In the previous chapters, I provided various data sources to assist Section 504 Coordinators. This chapter offers some **Essential Tips** for leading Section 504 and highlights character traits that positively impact change.

Tip 1: Resiliency will take you far, so empower resiliency. Working with humans in education and leadership will pull you in many directions. Be flexible when the uncontrollable happens, adapt, and demonstrate resiliency, purpose, and perseverance. Focus on the big picture and what you are trying to accomplish rather than the particulars. According to Allison, strong leaders understand the importance of resiliency in school leadership. These leaders: (1) engage in personal renewal; (2) ensure their words convey respect and inspiration; (3) stay optimistic; (4) blunt the impact of setbacks; (5) cultivate networks before a crisis; (6) see patterns revealed by data and use them to instigate change (Allison, 2011, 2012, p.79-82).

Tip 2: Model confidence and lead confidently in Section 504. As you lead Section 504, your confidence will influence others to follow or flee. Confidence serves as a solid foundation for one that is unshakable, resilient, and fearless. When you exhibit those qualities, you can influence others, guide them on a path, and build upon your solid foundation. Bandura (2000) explained that "when faced with obstacles, setbacks, and failures, those who doubt their capabilities slacken their efforts, give up, or settle for mediocre solutions. Those who strongly believe in the capabilities redouble their efforts to master the challenge" (p. 120).

Tip 3: Build a team and lead the team if you are the Section 504 Coordinator. Teamwork is defined by Scarnati (2001, p. 5) "as a cooperative process that allows ordinary people to achieve extraordinary results." Harris & Harris (1996) states that a team has a common goal or purpose where team members can develop effective, mutual relationships to achieve those goals. The common goal of the Section 504 coordinator is to ensure quality services for students with disabilities receiving services under Section 504.

Foster the team to provide a Free and Appropriate Education. Here are some essential characteristics for empowering teams:

1. Have a Vision: "Effective educational leaders help their schools to develop visions that embody the best thinking about teaching and learning" (Leithwood and Riehl, 2003, p.3). Take some time and decide what vision you want to make into a reality for your team.

2. Set Goals: Once you have a vision, decide what goal you want to accomplish related to the Section 504 role. Set small goals and build upon those goals.

3. Communicate Effectively: effective communication builds trust, clarifies the vision, and establishes loyalty within the

team. An early Harvard Business School study linked success and promotion with individuals who can effectively communicate, make sound decisions, and get things done with the help of others (Bowman et al., 1964). Effective communicating leaders adjust public speaking, specifically for the audience, which may vary from large groups, such as faculty meetings, to individual conversations with parents, teachers, and students (Lunenberg, 2010). Effective communication is a two-way process that requires effort and skill by both sender and receiver. Active listening is another key component of communication. Listen to the messages without passing judgment or giving advice, taking in and decoding the message's context, not the person.

4. Empower Others: Build your team and share your leadership with others, including teachers, while facilitating meetings and coordinating with others. Work with your Section 504 teams, identify these experts, and empower others with your knowledge and Section 504 expertise. Work to determine if team members have additional functions or talents and how this may be useful within the school building related to Section 504. If you are a leader, this may be easier. If you are a counselor or not in a supervisory role, you may have to solicit support from your leadership team to support you with empowering others.

5. Be trustworthy. Trust is particularly important for ongoing team success. As a Section 504 coordinator, it is important that you set an example by modeling and demonstrating

trust in your teachers and your administrative team. Trust is a phenomenon that requires intentional efforts and work from those involved in the process. A state of trust is not automatic. One develops trust based on one's actions (Kutsyuruba & Walker, 2015). Be trustworthy and work on trusting your team; foster reliable behaviors through sharing and communication.

6. Establish Norms: Set ground rules or standards to establish general team expectations and help maintain order and productivity.

7. Model: Practice what you preach and model teamwork, positivity, and professionalism. You are the Section 504 coordinator, and if you act like this role is a chore and you despise it, others will mirror your actions. Your attitudes and behaviors are contagious.

Tip 4: Seek Knowledge: Build knowledge and associate yourself with a Section 504 support team. Identify and build a team with skilled Section 504 contacts, stakeholders in your district, and other Section 504 leaders in neighboring schools. Collaborate with other leaders with general knowledge and experience. Exchange phone numbers emails, or create a community group using a professional network so you can have someone as a mentor and ask questions.

Tip 5: Exhale, take a step back, and then prioritize. Mentally adjust, then organize your thoughts. Decide what is essential to help you develop a local school Section 504 system that implements Section 504 services, provides FAPE, and facilitates task-driven outcomes. According to "Principals and Special Education: The Critical Role of School Leaders... Although principals do not need to be disability experts, they must have fundamental knowledge and skills to perform essential special education leadership tasks" (DiPaola & Walther-Thomas, 2003, p.11). Gain the fundamental knowledge and set up parameters to perform essential Section 504 coordinator tasks.

Tip 6: Change your Mindset: Our attitudes, energies, and demeanor often reveal positive thoughts and mindsets. "Mindsets are core sets of beliefs that become the lenses through which we see, interpret, and respond to the worlds within which we work and live" (Cherkowski, 2018, p.68; Dweck, 2006; Gergen, 2015; McGonigal, 2015). Mindsets are the way we perceive and respond. Flourishing and positive moods reflect an openness of mind, heart, and spirit to the joys, mysteries, and unlimited abundance (Cherkowski, Hanson & Walker, 2018).

Tip 7: Focus on the Positives: have a positive attitude and mindset. As a Section 504 Coordinator, your words, actions, thoughts, and feelings matter and influence others.

Tip 8: Reflect and learn from experiences: Reflect on the day's journey, learn from your mistakes, celebrate gains, and move forward. Whatever obstacles you face, you will pass, so do not waste too much time overanalyzing or criticizing yourself. Do things that make you happy, whether watching TV, journaling, spending time with family, exercising, praying, practicing mindful meditation, etc.

Tip 9: Establish a Self-Care Routine: Take time for yourself. Reward yourself. Always do things that fill up your bucket. Time is irreplaceable. Take time for yourself, and practice self-love. You are irreplaceable to family and friends, so keep things in perspective.

Tip 10: Follow all other tips and knowledge from reading this book. Allow this book to be a hands-on resource.

Section 504 Coordinators lead and facilitate meetings. Combative or litigious meetings are not always easy and can be emotionally draining. Nonetheless, as the Section 504 Coordinator, it is your role to facilitate and navigate such meetings.

Here are some **Essential Tips** for challenging meetings based on my experience:
- Inform your school administrator about the situation so they know the problem.
- Seek district or administrative guidance before the meeting to brainstorm outcomes.
- Hold a Preparatory Activity Meeting- where the school team meets before the meeting without parents to review progress, assign roles, address concerns, and discuss pertinent information (without predetermining).
- During the Preparatory Meetings, discuss:
  ➢ Current academics

> - Behavior data
> - Use of accommodations
> - Teacher input, recommendations, and observations
> - Current universal screeners and standardized test scores
> - Recent evaluations or medical information
> - Any relevant notes or emails.

- Use the seven-step process from Chapter Eight (Ethical Leadership) to navigate outcomes.
- Seat everyone strategically (if there are conflicts between parents/teachers, space everyone out accordingly).
- Set Norms (ground rules for the meeting)
- Have a set plan or agenda (include a beginning and end time)-Send it to the parent ahead of time with roles such as a note-taker, timekeeper, and technology navigator.
- Remain calm when emotions arise or take breaks.
- Remain professional and refrain from becoming defensive or taking things personally. (Remain poised even when the going gets tough).
- Remain student-focused and data-driven.
- Stick to the schedule and redirect distractions or comments.
- Prepare for an additional meeting if time is running out. Set a hard end time so that the team can reconvene another day.
- As the Section 504 Coordinator, be prepared to offer the final offer of a Free and Appropriate Education on behalf of the team.

- Have a plan to resolve issues. Think globally and strategically.
- If you are religious (Pray before the meeting), prayer changes things.

Essentially, be prepared and communicate effectively. Remain professional. Emotions may run high during challenging meetings. As the LEA, you are the facilitator, and your role is to lead the Section 504 team with integrity and collectively. Your goal as the LEA is to build consensus, remain professional, and support your teachers, parents, and personnel as a cohesive team that helps students with disabilities under Section 504 and offers a Free and Appropriate Public Education.

"Conscious purpose leads to goals. Goals lead to intention. Intention leads to commitment. Commitment generates enthusiasm. Enthusiasm produces energy. Energy leads to achievement." Michael Josephson

CONCLUSION:
THE WORLD OF SECTION 504 IS YOURS

"Let nothing be done in your life which will cause you to fear if it becomes known." Epicurus

I hope this book provides valuable insight into Section 504 and the role that Section 504 coordinators play in providing equitable services for students with disabilities. Books and classes are great resources. However, nothing is as impactful as hands-on experiences and lessons learned while in the position.

I say all of this to say that the world of Section 504 is yours for the taking. Be intentional and take immediate action to secure the role. I understand it can be overwhelming, but you must start somewhere. Be resilient and use your knowledge of Section 504 to impact change positively. Be the change and work step by step to shift the culture in your building to one of empowerment and inclusion.

Advocate for students with disabilities. You have read about the history and the climb for inclusion and equality for students with disabilities. Focus on that history of discrimination to promote the future of equity and inclusion in the school and community. While fostering and promoting inclusion, continue to build those relationships and navigate the waters on all levels.

Section 504 is multifaceted, so solid relationships with students, families, communities, stakeholders, and school personnel will take you far. Be active, seize the moments, and coordinate with others. Honor your Section 504 coordinator roles and responsibilities, lead with your heart, and remain ethical. Use these tips and make them your own to build Section 504 capacity and impact change. Change does not happen overnight; small steps can lead to significant outcomes. Trust me and trust the process.

In conclusion, take this opportunity and knowledge and create your narrative and journey. Although working with laws, students with disabilities, and compliance can feel overwhelming and daunting, you have the skill set to provide services and make things happen. As the author and fellow educator, I believe in you. Your principal also believes in you, which is why you have been designated to fulfill this role. Believe it or not, the Section 504 coordinator role can be extremely rewarding. Whether this is temporary or permanent, people and families have faith and depend on you to make a difference. GO FORTH AND LEAD because failure is not an option!

"It always seems impossible until it's done."
Nelson Mandela

ABOUT THE AUTHOR

Dr. Nakia S. Cotton resides in Marietta, Georgia, with her two sons. She has twenty-seven years of education experience and fourteen years of leadership experience in special education, Section 504, Response to Intervention/MTSS, and English Speakers of Other Languages. Dr. Cotton is a graduate of Florida A&M University and Clark Atlanta University. She currently serves as a Supervisor in Special Education in the Atlanta Metro Area. Dr. Cotton is the owner of Edufaith Educational Services. If you would like Section 504 or Special Education training, consultations, or school or district support, contact me at

www.edufaithconsulting.com

REFERENCES

Alexander, T. M. (2014). Teacher-student relationships and academic achievement (Doctoral dissertation, Walden University).

All About Vision Editorial Team. (2021, January 20). What is low vision? All About Vision. https://www.allaboutvision.com/lowvision/

Allison, E. (Dec 2011-Jan. 2012). The Resilient Leader. Educational Leadership. Volume 69(4). 79-82

Allison, E., & Reeves, D. (2011). Renewal coaching field guide: How effective leaders sustain meaningful change. San Francisco: Jossey-Bass.

American Cancer Society. (n.d.). What Is Cancer? https://www.cancer.org/cancer/cancer-basics/what-is-cancer.html

AMERICANS WITH DISABILITIES ACT OF 1990, AS AMENDED. (n.d.). Retrieved February 2, 2021, from https://www.ada.gov/pubs/ada.htm

Anderman, E. M. (2002). School effects on psychological outcomes during adolescence. Journal of Educational Psychology, 94(4), 795–809. https://doi.org/10.1037/0022-0663.94.4.795

Andrews, D., & Lewis, M. (2004). Building sustainable futures: Emerging understandings of the significant contribution of the professional learning community. Improving Schools, 7(2), 129-150. doi:10.1177/1365480204047345

Angelou, M. (2013). I've learned that people will forget what you said, people will forget what you did, but people will never forget how you made them feel.

Anorexia nervosa - Symptoms and causes. (n.d.). Mayo Clinic. https://www.mayoclinic.org/diseases-conditions/anorexia-nervosa/symptoms-causes/syc-20353591

Autism Speaks. (n.d.). What Is Autism? https://www.autismspeaks.org/what-autism

Bandura, A. (2000). Exercise of human agency through collective efficacy. Current directions in psychological science, 9(3), 75-78.

Bandura, A. (2000). Cultivate self-efficacy for personal and organizational effectiveness. Handbook of principles of organizational behavior, 2, 0011-21.

Barton, Paul E. 2003. Parsing the Achievement Gap: Baselines for Tracking Progress. Princeton, NJ: Policy Information Report, Educational Testing Service.

Barth, R. (1990). Improving schools from within. San Francisco: Jossey Bass. Google Scholar

Bateman, D., & Bateman, C. F. (2001). A principal's guide to special education. Arlington, VA: Council for Exceptional Children.

Baer, R. A., Smith, G. T., Hopkins, J., Krietemeyer, J., & Toney, L. (2006). Using self-report assessment methods to explore facets of mindfulness. Assessment, 13, 27-45.

Baer, R. A. & Krietemeyer, J. (2006). Overview of mindfulness and acceptance-based treatment approaches. In R. A. Baer (Ed.), Mindfulness-based treatment approaches Clinician's guide to evidence base and applications (pp. 3-27). San Diego, CA: Elsevier.

Barrett, D.J. (2006). Leadership Communication. (New York: McGraw-Hill, 2006). The definition of and model for leadership communication are based on this book.

Barth, R. S. (1990). Improving schools from within: Teachers, parents, and principals can make the difference. Jossey-Bass Inc., Publishers, 350 Sansome Street, San Francisco, CA 94104-1310.

Bennis, W., & Nanus, B. (1985). Leadership: The strategies for taking charge: New York: Harper & Row.

Benz, M. R., Lindstrom, L., & Yovanoff, P. (2000). Improving graduation and employment outcomes of students with disabilities: Predictive factors and student perspectives. Exceptional Children, 66, 509-29.

Billingsley, B. S. (1993). Teacher retention and attrition in special education: A critical review of the literature. Journal of Special Education, 27, 137-174.

Billingsley, B. S., & Cross, L. H. (1991). Teachers' decisions to transfer from special to general education. Journal of Special Education, 24, 496-511.

Bolman, L., & Deal, T. (1996). Leading with soul. San Francisco, CA: Jossey-Bass. Google Scholar

Bolman, L. G., & Deal, T. E. (1992). Leading and managing: Effects of context, culture, and gender. Educational administration quarterly, 28(3), 314-329.

Bolman, L. G., & Deal, T. E. (2017). Reframing organizations: Artistry, choice, and leadership. John Wiley & Sons.

Bolman, Lee G., and Terrence E. Deal. "Leading and managing: Effects of context, culture, and gender." Educational administration quarterly 28, no.3 (1992): 314-329.

Board of Education of Hendrick Hudson Central School District v. Rowley, 458 U.S. 176 (1982).

Bowman, G.W., Jones, L.W., Peterson, R.A., Gronouski, J.A., & Mahoney, R.M. (1964). What helps or harms promotability? Harvard Business Review. 42 (1), pp. 6-18.

Bracey, H. (2002). Building trust. How to get it. How to keep it. Taylorsville, GA: HB Artworks.

Brookover, W., Beamer, L., Efthim, H., Hathaway, D., Lezotte, L., Miller, S., et al. (1982). Creating effective schools. Holmes Beach, FL: Learning Publications.

Brougher, C. (2010). Section 504 of the Rehabilitation Act of 1973: Prohibiting Discrimination Against Individuals with Disabilities in Programs or Activities Receiving Federal Assistance.

Brougher, C. (2012, March 22). The Americans with Disabilities Act (ADA): Statutory Language and Recent Issues. CRS Reports. https://www.everycrsreport.com/reports/98-921.html

Brougher, C. (2011). The Individuals with Disabilities Education Act (IDEA): Statutory Provisions and Recent Legal Issues. Congressional Research Service. https://www.everycrsreport.com/files/20110511_R40690_d76ca0406a3db630ff 94a4a64063c87c24cc55c6.pdf

Brown v. Board of Education of Topeka, Kansas, 347 U.S. 483 (1954). Retrieved from: https://www.history.com/topics/black-history/brown-v-board-of-education-of-topeka

Brown, M. E., Trevino, L. K., & Harrison, D. A. (2005). Ethical leadership: A social learning perspective for construct development and testing. Organizational Behavior and Human Decision Processes, 97(2), 117-134.

Brownell, M. T., & Smith, S. W. (1993). Understanding special education attrition: A conceptual model and implications for teacher education. Teacher Education and Special Education, 16, 270-282.

Cherkowski, S., Hanson, K., & Walker, K. (2018). Mindful alignment: Foundations of educator flourishing. Lexington Books.

Christenson, S., & Sheridan, S. M. (Eds.). (2001). Schools and families: Creating essential connections for learning. Guilford Press.

Coleman, J. S. (1990). Foundations of social theory. Cambridge, MA: Belknap Press of Harvard University Press.

Confidence. (n.d.). Retrieved November 02, 2019, from https://www.merriam webster.com/dictionary/confidence

Connors, Neila A. (2000). If you don't feed the teachers, they eat the students: Guide to success for administrators and teachers: Nashville, TN: Incentive Publications.

Cooke, M. (2011, October 11). 2011 CEA Pat Clifford Award Winner: Positive teacher-student relationships play a unique role for students with special needs. Retrieved January 07, 2011, from CEA: http://www.cea-ace.ca/press-release/2011-cea-patclifford-award-winner-positive-teacher-student-relationships-play-unique

Council for Exceptional Children [CEC]. (1994). Creating schools for all of our students: What 12 schools have to say. Reston, VA: Author.

Council for Exceptional Children. (1997). IDEA 1997: Let's make it work— Arlington, VA: Author.

Csorba, L. (2004). Trust: The one thing that makes or breaks a leader. Nelson Books.

Cyert, R. M. (1990). Defining leadership and explicating the process. Nonprofit Management & Leadership, 1(1), 29-38.

Danielson, C. (2006). Teacher leadership that strengthens professional practice. Alexandria VA: ASCD

Deal, T. E., & Peterson, K. D. (1990). The principal's role in shaping school culture. US Department of Education, Office of Educational Research, and Improvement.

De Valenzuela, J. S., Copeland, S. R., Qi, C. H., & Park, M. (2006). Examining educational equity: Revisiting the disproportionate representation of minority students in special education. Exceptional Children, 72(4), 425–441.

DiPaola, M. F., Walther-Thomas, C. (2003). Principals and special education: The critical role of school leaders (COPPSE Document No. IB-7). Gainesville, FL: the University of Florida, Center on Personnel Studies in Special Education.

Disability Secrets Homepage. (n.d.). Www.Disabilitysecrets.Com. https://www.disabilitysecrets.com/

Dirks, K. T., & Ferrin, D. L. (2002). Trust in leadership: Meta-analytic findings and implications for research and practice—Journal of applied psychology, 87(4), 611.

DuFour, R., & Marzano, R. J. (2011). Leaders of learning: How district, school, and classroom leaders improve student achievement. Solution Tree Press.

Dweck, C. (2016). What having a "growth mindset" Actually Means. Harvard Business Review, 13, 213-226.

Edmonds, R. (1979). Effective schools for the urban poor. Educational leadership, 37(1), 15-24.

Eggert, D. & Minutelli, A.M (2012). The Role and Responsibility of the LEA Representative. Retrieved from: http://www.wadleighlaw.com/wp-content/uploads/dlm_uploads/2015/02/LEA-Representative-The-Role-and-Responsibility-of-the.pdf

Embich, J. L. (2001). The relationship of secondary special education teachers' roles and factors that lead to professional burnout. Teacher Education and Special Education, 24, 58-69.

Esteves, Kelli J., and Rao, Shaila, "The Evolution of Special Education" (2008).

Scholarship and Professional Work – Education. 72. https://digitalcommons.butler.edu/coe_papers/72

Fibromyalgia - Symptoms, and causes. (2020, October 7). Mayo Clinic. https://www.mayoclinic.org/diseases-conditions/fibromyalgia/symptoms-causes/syc-20354780

Friend, M., & Cook, L. (2003). Interactions: Collaboration Skills for School Professionals (4th ed.). Boston, MA: Allyn and Bacon.

Fullan, Michael. (1997). What's worth fighting for in the principalship. New York: Teachers College Press.

Function Abilities. (n.d.). What Are Processing Disorders? Retrieved from https://www.makingtherapyfun.com/conditions-we-treat/processing-disorders/

Galford, R. M., & Drapeau, A. S. (2003). The trusted leader. Simon and Schuster.

Gartner, A., & Lipsky, D.K. (1987). Beyond special education: Toward a quality system for all students. Harvard Educational Review, 57, 367-395.

Geller, M., Einstein, A., Holmes Jr, O. W., & Trujillo, E. J. Find your Passion.

Gergen, K. (1999/2015). An invitation to social construction (3rd Ed). Thousand Oaks, CA: Sage.

Gersten, R., Keating, T., Yovanoff, P., & Harniss, M. K. (2001). Working in special education: Factors that enhance special educators' intent to stay. Exceptional Children, 67, 549-553.

Greenleaf, R. (2015, March 26). Share Your Story - Leading from the Heart. Greenleaf Center for Servant Leadership. https://www.greenleaf.org/leading-from-the-heart/

Greenfield, William D., Jr. "Rationale and Methods To Articulate Ethics and Administrator Training." Paper presented at the annual meeting of the American Educational Research Association, Chicago, April 1991. 32 pages. ED332 379

Greeson, J. M. (2009). Mindfulness research update: 2008. Complementary health practice review, 14(1), 10-18.

Gronn, P. (2002). Distributed leadership. In K. Leithwood, P. Hallinger, K. Seashore-Louis, G. Furman-Brown, P. Gronn, W. Mulford, & K. Riley (Eds.), Second International Handbook of Educational Leadership and Administration (pp. 653-696). Dordrecht, NL: Kluwer. doi:10.1007/978-94-010-0375-9_23

Gruenert, S. (2005). Correlations of collaborative school cultures and student achievement. NASSP Bulletin, 89(645), 43-55.

Gunderson, L. (2000). Voices of the teenage diasporas. Journal of Adolescent and Adult Literacy, 43(8), 692-7.

Hallinger, P. (1996). Challenging and changing Primrose. Prime Focus, 2(4), 20–

29.Google Scholar

Hallinger, P., & Heck, R. H. (1996). Reassessing the principal's role in school effectiveness: A review of empirical research, 1980-1995. Educational administration quarterly, 32(1), 5-44.

Hallinger, P., & Heck, R. H. (2002). What do you call people with visions? The role of vision, mission, and goals in school leadership and improvement. In Second international handbook of educational leadership and administration (pp. 9-40). Springer, Dordrecht.

Hardman, M. L., & Nagle, K. (2004). Public policy: From access to accountability in special education. Critical issues in special education: Access, diversity, and accountability, 277-292.

Hardman, M. L., & Nagle, K. (2004). Public policy. In A. McCray Sorrells, H. Rieth, & P. T. Sindelar (Eds.), Critical issues in special education (pp. 277-291). Boston: Pearson Education.

Harris, P. R., & Harris, K. G. (1996). Managing effectively through teams. Team Performance Management: An International Journal, 2(3), 23-36.

Health, N. I. (2021, May 19). NIMH » Anxiety Disorders. National Institute of Mental Health. https://www.nimh.nih.gov/health/topics/anxiety-disorders/

Healthy Place. (2019, August 7). What Are Emotional and Behavioral Disorders? | Healthy Place. https://www.healthyplace.com/parenting/behavior-disorders/what-are-emotional-and-behavioral-disorders

Hitt, W. D. (1990). Ethics and leadership: Putting theory into practice. Columbus: Battelle Press.

Honig, B. (1984). School reform is working: What's wrong with goal setting and measurement. San Jose Mercury, 1c, 2c.

Howey, K. R. (1988). Why teacher leadership? Journal of Teacher Education, 39(1), 28-31. doi:10.1177/002248718803900107

Impairment https://www.merriam-webster.com/dictionary/impairment. (n.d.). In Merriam-Webster. Retrieved from https://www.merriam-webster.com/dictionary/impairment

Individuals with Disabilities Education Act, 20 U.S.C. §§ 1400 et seq. (2005).

Individuals with Disabilities Education Act regulations. (2006, August 14). Federal Register, 71, 46, 540. et seq

Jansen, E., & Von Glinow, M. A. (1985). Ethical ambivalence and organizational reward systems. Academy of Management Review, 814-822.

Jeynes, W.H. 2003. A meta-analysis: The effects of parental involvement on minority children's academic achievement. Education & Urban Society 35(2): 202-218.

Journey. (n.d.). The Merriam-Webster.Com Dictionary. Retrieved July 5, 2018, from https://www.merriam-webster.com/dictionary/journey

Katsiyannis, A., Conderman, G., & Franks, D. J. (1996). State practices on inclusion: A national review. Remedial and Special Education, 16, 279-287.

Kabat-Zinn, J., & Hanh, T. N. (2009). Full catastrophe living: Using the wisdom of your body and mind to face stress, pain, and illness. New York, NY: Bantam Books.

Kearns, J. F., Kleinert, H. L., & Clayton, J. (1998). Principal supports for inclusive assessment: A Kentucky story. Teaching Exceptional Children, 31(2), 16-23.

Kellison, Michael. (2007). Transforming a school into a community. Principal, 86(5), 58-59.

Keijzer, P. (2019, October 15). Is It Better To Lead With Your Heart Or Your Head? Retrieved from https://www.business2community.com/leadership/is-it-better-to-lead-with-your-heart-or-your-head-02249815

Killion, J., & Harrison, C. (2006). Taking the lead: New roles for teachers and school-based coaches. Oxford, OH : National Staff Development Council

Kidder, Rushworth M. How Good People Make Tough Choices. New York: William Morrow, 1995.

Kirby, Peggy C.; Louis V. Pardise; and Russell Protti. "The Ethical Reasoning of School Administrators:

The Principled Principal." Paper presented at the annual meeting of the American Educational Research

Association, Boston, April 1990. 11 pages. ED320 253

Kouzes, J. M., & Posner, B. Z. (2006). The leadership challenge (Vol. 3). John Wiley & Sons.

Kupper, L. (2000). A Guide to the Individualized Education Program.

Kutsyuruba, B. & Walker, K (2015) The lifecycle of trust in educational leadership: an ecological perspective, International Journal of Leadership in Education, 18:1, 106-121, DOI: 10.1080/13603124.2014.915061 To link to this article: https://doi.org/10.1080/13603124.2014.915061

Kutsyuruba, B., & Walker, K. (2013). Ethical challenges in school administration: Perspectives of Canadian principals. Organizational Cultures, 12(3), 85-99.

Lashway, L. (1996). Ethical Leadership. Eric Digest, 107, 1–5.

Laurence, B. A. K. (n.d.). Getting Social Security Disability for Peripheral Neuropathy. Www.Disabilitysecrets.Com. https://www.disabilitysecrets.com/social-security-disability-neuropathy.html

Leithwood, K. (1994). Leadership for school restructuring. Educational administration quarterly, 30(4), 498-518.

Leithwood, K. A., & Riehl, C. (2003). What we know about successful school leadership. Nottingham: National College for School Leadership.

Leithwood, K., & Jantzi, D. (1990). Transformational leadership: How principals can help reform school cultures. School Effectiveness and School Improvement, 1(4), 249-280.

Leithwood, K. A., & Poplin, M. (1992, February). The move toward transformational leadership. Educational Leadership, 49(5), 8.

Leithwood, K. (2005). Educational leadership: A review of the research. Philadelphia, PA: The Mid-Atlantic Regional Educational Laboratory at Temple University. Retrieved from www.temple.edu/lss

Livingston, C. (1992). Introduction: Teacher leadership for restructured schools. In C. Livingston (Ed.), Teachers as leaders: Evolving roles (pp. 9-17). NEA School Restructuring Series. Washington, DC: National Education Association.

Louis, K. S., Leithwood, K., Wahlstrom, K. L., & Anderson, S. E. (2010). Investigating the links to improved student learning: Final report of research findings. St. Paul, MN: University of Minnesota.

Lunenburg, Fred. (2010). Communication: The Process, Barriers, And Improving Effectiveness. Volume 1, Number 1

Mandela, N. (2014). Education is the most powerful weapon which you can use to change the world. Computer, 8, 45pm.

Mandela, N. (2017). It always seems impossible until it's done.

Marsh, L., McGee, R., & Williams, S. (2014). School Climate and Aggression among New Zealand High School Students. New Zealand Journal of Psychology, 43(1).

Marzano, R.J., Waters, T., & McNulty, B.A. (2005). School leadership that works: From results to research. Alexandria, VA: Association for Supervision and Curriculum Development.

Mawhinney, T. S., & Sagan, L. L. (2007). The power of personal relationships. Phi Delta Kappan, 88(6), 460-464.

Mayo Clinic. (2017, July 22). Dyslexia - Symptoms and causes. https://www.mayoclinic.org/diseases-conditions/dyslexia/symptoms-causes/syc-20353552

Mayo Clinic. (2018, July 6). Post-traumatic stress disorder (PTSD) - Symptoms and causes. https://www.mayoclinic.org/diseases-conditions/post-traumatic-stress-disorder/symptoms-causes/syc-20355967

Mayo Clinic. (2020a, February 22). Concussion - Symptoms, and causes.

https://www.mayoclinic.org/diseases-conditions/concussion/symptoms-causes/syc-20355594

Mayo Clinic. (2020b, October 7). Fibromyalgia - Symptoms, and causes. https://www.mayoclinic.org/diseases-conditions/fibromyalgia/symptoms-causes/syc-20354780

Mayo Clinic. (2020c, November 6). Narcolepsy - Symptoms and causes. https://www.mayoclinic.org/diseases-conditions/narcolepsy/symptoms-causes/syc-20375497

Mayo Clinic. (2021, February 4). Traumatic brain injury - symptoms and causes. https://www.mayoclinic.org/diseases-conditions/traumatic-brain-injury/symptoms-causes/syc-20378557

Medical Conditions - Eligibility for Disability Benefits. (n.d.). Www.Disabilitysecrets.Com. https://www.disabilitysecrets.com/topics/medical-conditions-eligibility-disability-benefits

Migraine - Symptoms and causes. (2020, January 16). Mayo Clinic. https://www.mayoclinic.org/diseases-conditions/migraine-headache/symptoms-causes/syc-20360201

McCormick, M. J. (2001). Self-efficacy and leadership effectiveness: Applying social cognitive theory to leadership. Journal of Leadership Studies, 8(1), 22-33.

McGonigal, K. (2015). The upside of stress: Why stress is good for you and how to get good at it. New York, NY: Penguin.

Mihelic, K. K., Lipicnik, B., & Tekavcic, M. (2010). Ethical leadership. International Journal of Management & Information Systems (IJMIS), 14(5).

Moore, Catherine (2020, October 13). What is Mindfulness? Positives and Benefits: Positive Psychology.com https://positivepsychology.com/what-is-mindfulness/

Miller, M. D., Brownell, M. T., & Smith, S. W. (1999). Factors that predict teachers staying in, leaving, or transferring from the special education classroom. Exceptional Children, 65, 201-218.

Meyer, L. M. (2000). Barriers to meaningful instruction for English learners. Theory Into Practice, 39(4), 228-236.

Nappi, J. S. (2014). The teacher leader: Improving schools by building social capital through shared leadership. Delta Kappa Gamma Bulletin, 80(4).

National Association of Elementary School Principals (1998). Early childhood education and the elementary school principal: Standards for quality programs for young children. (ERIC Document Reproduction Service Number 450466.

National Association of Elementary School Principals & ILIAD Project. (2001). Implementing IDEA: A guide for principals. Arlington, VA: Council for

Exceptional Children and Alexandria, VA: National Association of Elementary School Principals.

National Association of Elementary School Principals [NAESP] (2001a). Essentials for

principals: School leader's guide to special education. Alexandria, VA: Author.

National Education Association. (2008). Parent, Family, Community Involvement in Education. Retrieved August 17, 2016, from NEA Education Policy and Practice Department, http://www.nea.org/assets/docs/PB11_ParentInvolvement08.pdf.

National Association of Elementary School Principal [NAESP]. (2001b). Leading learning communities: NAESP standards for What Principals Should Know and be able to Do. Retrieved from: https://www.naesp.org/sites/default/files/resources/1/Pdfs/LLC2-ES.pdf

NAESP. (2002). The Principal's Creed. Retrieved on October 8, 2002, from www.NAESP.org/principalscreed.

NASDSE: National Association of State Directors of Special Education. (2006). Response to Intervention: Policy consideration and implementation. Alexandria, VA: Author.

National Institute for Mental Health. (n.d.). NIMH » Bipolar Disorder. https://www.nimh.nih.gov/health/topics/bipolar-disorder/

NIMH » Anxiety Disorders. (n.d.). Anxiety Disorders. Retrieved May 19, 2021, from https://www.nimh.nih.gov/health/topics/anxiety-disorders/

National Museum of American History. (2015, July 8). Sitting-in for disability rights: The Section 504 protests of the. https://americanhistory.si.edu/blog/sitting-disability-rights-section-504-protests-1970s

NOLO Press. (n.d.-b). Medical Conditions. Disability Secrets. https://www.disabilitysecrets.com/topics/medical-conditions-eligibility-disability-benefits

Office for Civil Rights, senior staff memorandum, 19 IDELR 894 (1992).

Office of Special Education Services. (2015). Retrieved from: https://www2.ed.gov/pubs/OSEP95AnlRpt/ch1c.html

Office of Special Education (2020). Retrieved from: https://www2.ed.gov/pubs/OSEP95AnlRpt/ch1b.html

Osher, T. (1997). IDEA Reauthorized—a role for families enhanced. Claiming Children, 1-8.

Paglis, L. L., & Green, S. G. (2002). Both sides now: Supervisor and subordinate perspectives on relationship quality. Journal of Applied Social Psychology, 32(2),

250-276.

Paglis, L. L., & Green, S. G. (2002). Leadership self-efficacy and managers' motivation for leading change. Journal of Organizational Behavior: The International Journal of Industrial, Occupational and Organizational Psychology and Behavior, 23(2), 215-235.

Pankake, A. M., & Fullwood, H. L. (1999). "Principals of inclusion;" Things they need to know and do. Catalyst for Change, 28, 25-26.

Parker, S. A., & Day, V. P. (1997, March). Promoting inclusion through instructional leadership: The roles of the secondary school principal. NASSP Bulletin, 83-89.

Payne, S (2020). Public Law 94-142. https://www3.nd.edu/~rbarger/www7/pl94-142.html

Pauley, J. A. (2010). Communication: The key to effective leadership. Milwaukee, WI: ASQ Quality Press.

Peterson, T. (2019, August 7). What Are Emotional and Behavioral Disorders?, Healthy Place. Retrieved on 2021, March 6 from https://www.healthyplace.com/parenting/behavior-disorders/what-are-emotional-and-behavioral-disorders

Phippen, J. W. (2015, July 6). The racial imbalances of special education. The Atlantic. Retrieved from: https://www.theatlantic.com/education/archive/2015/07/the-racial-imbalances-of-special-education/397775/

Protecting Students with Disabilities. (n.d.-b). Retrieved from https://www2.ed.gov/about/offices/list/ocr/504faq.html

Pulliam, J. D., & Van Patten, J. J. (2006). History of education in America (9th ed.). Upper Saddle River, NJ: Pearson Education.

Purkey, S. C., & Smith, M. S. (1985). Educational policy and school effectiveness. Research on exemplary schools (pp. 181-200). Academic Press.

Reeves, D. B., & Allison, E. (2009). Renewal Coaching: Sustainable change for individuals and organizations. San Francisco: Jossey-Bass.

Reeves, D. B., & Allison, E. (2010). Renewal coaching workbook. San Francisco: Jossey-Bass.

Rey, R.B., Smith, A.L., Yoon, J., Somers, C., & Barnett, D. (2007). Relationships between teacher and urban African American children. School Psychology International, 28, 346-364.

Rieg, S. A. (2007). Principals and young children: A dozen recommendations for building positive relationships. Early Childhood Education Journal, 35(3), 209-213.

Rock, M. L., Thead, B. K., Gable, R. A., Hardman, M. L., & Van Acker, R. (2006). In pursuit of excellence: The past as prologue to a brighter future for special education. Focus on exceptional children, 38(8), 1-18.

Rosenthal, R., & Jacobson, L. (1968). Pygmalion in the classroom: Teacher expectation and pupils' intellectual development. New York: Holt, Rinehart & Winston.

Rosenthal, R., & Jacobson, L. (2000). Teacher expectations for the disadvantaged. In P. K. Smith, & A. D. Pellegrini (Eds.), Psychology of education: Major themes (pp. 286-291). Routledgefalmer: London

Sage, D., & Burello, L. (1994). Leadership in educational reform: An administrator's guide to changes in special education. Baltimore, MD: Paul H. Brooks.

Scarnati, J. T. (2001). On becoming a team player. Team Performance Management: An International Journal, 7(1/2), 5-10.

Servant leaders lead with mind and heart. (n.d.). Https://Www.Linkedin.Com/Pulse/Servant-Leaders-Lead-Mind-Heart-Ms-Jemi-Sudhakar/. https://www.linkedin.com/pulse/servant-leaders-lead-mind-heart-ms-jemi-sudhakar/

Sergiovanni, Thomas J. Moral Leadership: Getting to the Heart of School Leadership. San Francisco:

Jossey-Bass, 1992.

Sichel, Betty A. "Ethics Committees and Teacher Ethics." In Ethics for Professionals in Education:

Perspectives for Preparation and Practice, edited by Kenneth Strike and P. Lance Ternasky. 162-75.

New York: Teachers College Press, 1993.

Starratt, Robert J. "Building an Ethical School: A Theory for Practice in Educational Leadership."

Educational Administration Quarterly 27, 2 (May 1991): 185-202. EJ425 540

Shields, Carolyn M. (2006). Creating spaces for value-based conversations: The role of school leaders in the 21st century. International Studies in Educational Administration 34(2), 62-81.

Short Bowel Syndrome. (n.d.). National Institute of Diabetes and Digestive and Kidney Diseases. https://www.niddk.nih.gov/health-information/digestive-diseases/short-bowel-syndrome

Sims, R. R. (1992). The challenge of ethical behavior in organizations. Journal of Business Ethics, 11(7), 505-513.

Smalley, S.L. & Winston, D. (2010). Fully present: The science, art, and practice of mindfulness.

Philadelphia, PA: De Capo Press.

Smith, J. D. (2004). The historical contexts of special education. Critical issues in special education, 1-14.

Smith, J. D. (2004). The historical contexts of special education: Framing our understanding of contemporary issues. Critical issues in special education: Access, diversity, and accountability, 1-15.

Sorrells, A. M., Reith, H. J., & Sindelar, P. T. (2004). Critical issues in special education. Boston, MA: Allyn & Bacon Inc.

Sparks, S. (2019). Why Teacher-Student Relationships Matter. Education Week. Vol. 38, Issue 25, Page 8 Retrieved from: https://www.edweek.org/ew/articles/2019/03/13/why-teacher-student-relationships-matter.html?print=1

Specific Learning Disabilities. (n.d.). Project IDEAL. http://www.projectidealonline.org/v/specific-learning-disabilities.

Stearns, P. N. (1998). Why study History. American Historical Association, 1-7.

Stockall, N., & Dennis, L. (2015). Seven Basic Steps to Solving Ethical Dilemmas in Special Education: A Decision-Making Framework. Education and Treatment of Children, 38(3), 329-344. Retrieved May 25, 2021, from http://www.jstor.org/stable/44684069

Tschannen-Moran, M., & Gareis, C. R. (2004). Principals' sense of efficacy. Journal of Educational Administration.

Toste, J. R. Heath, N. L. and Dallaire, L. (2010) "Perceptions of Classroom Working Alliance and Student Performance," Alberta Journal of Educational Research 56: 371-387. Retrieved from http://ajer.synergiesprairies.ca/

Turnbull, A., & Turnbull, R. (2001). Self-determination for individuals with significant cognitive disabilities and their families. Journal of the Association for Persons with Severe Handicaps, 26(1), 56-62.

Turnbull, A. P., & Turnbull, H. R. (2001). Families, professionals, and exceptionality: Collaborating for empowerment. Prentice-Hall.

Turner, Jamie S. (2007). Breaking the spell of the wicked principal. Principal, 87(2), 60-61.

Ujifusa, A. (2020, December 29). Sure, We Teach History. But Do We Know Why It's Important? Education Week. https://www.edweek.org/teaching-learning/sure-we-teach-history-but-do-we-know-why-its-important/2020/01

US Department of Education. (n.d.). A Guide to the Individualized Education

Program. Laws and Guidance: Special Education and Rehabilitation Programs. Retrieved November 19, 2020, from https://www2.ed.gov/parents/needs/speced/iepguide/index.html

US Department of Education. (n.d.). ED.gov. ED.Gov. https://www2.ed.gov/about/offices/list/ocr/docs/hq5269.html).

U.S. Department of Education. (2006). IDEA Part C Program Settings. Retrieved January 21, 2018, from www.ed.gov

US Department of Education. (2020). The IEP Process. Retrieved from: https://www2.ed.gov/parents/needs/speced/iepguide/index.html

US Department of Education. (n.d.) Archived: Thirty-five Years of Progress in Educating Children with Disabilities Through IDEA-- Pg. 10. Retrieved from https://www2.ed.gov/about/offices/list/osers/idea35/history/index_pg10.html

US Department of Education. (n.d.-a). Protecting Students with Disabilities. Retrieved from https://www2.ed.gov/about/offices/list/ocr/504faq.html

US Department of Education (2020). Office of Elementary and Secondary Education Local Education Agencies. Retrieved from: https://oese.ed.gov/offices/office-of-formula-grants/school-support-and-accountability/well-rounded-education-student-centered-funding-demonstration-grants/eligibility/

U.S. Department of Education, Office for Civil Rights. (2016). Civil Rights Data Collection: 2013–2014 State and National Estimations. Retrieved from: https://ocrdata.ed.gov/StateNationalEstimations/Estimations_2013_14

US Department of Education. (2017). Questions and Answers (Q&A) on US Supreme Court Case Decision Endrew F. v. Douglas County School District Re-1.

US Equal Employment Opportunity Commission. (n.d.). Retrieved from https://www.eeoc.gov/laws/guidance/questions-and-answers-final-rule-implementing-ada-amendments-act-2008

Valente, W. D. (1998). Law in the schools (4th ed.). Upper Saddle River, NJ: Merrill/Prentice Hall

Vergés, A. (2010). Integrating contextual issues in ethical decision making. Ethics & Behavior, 20(6), 497–507. http://dx.doi.org/10.1080/10508422.2010.52145

Vygotsky, L. S. (1978). Mind in Society. Cambridge, MA: Harvard University Press

Vygotsky, L. S. (1978). Mind in society. Cambridge, MA: Harvard University Press.

Vygotsky, L. S. (1962). Thought and language (E. Hanfmann & G. Vakar, Eds. and Trans.). Cambridge, MA: MIT Press. (Original work published 1934).

Wallace Foundation. (2012, January). The school principal as a leader: Guiding

schools to better teaching and learning. New York: Author. Retrieved from www.
wallacefoundation.org/knowledge-center/school-leadership/ effective-principal-
leadership/Pages/fte-School-Principal-as- Leader-Guiding-Schools-to-Better-
Teaching-and-Learning. Aspx

Wasley, P., Hampel, R., & Clark, R. (1997). The puzzle of whole-school change.
Phi Delta Kappan, 78, 690-697.

Waters, S. K., D. Cross, and T. Shaw. 2010. "How Important Are School and
Interpersonal Student Characteristics in Determining Later Adolescent School
Connectedness, by School Sector?" Australian Journal of Education 54 (2): 223–
243.

WebMD. (2016, October 18). What Is Dyscalculia? What Should I Do If My Child
Has It? https://www.webmd.com/add-adhd/childhood-adhd/dyscalculia-facts

Wells, C. M. (2013). Principals responding to constant pressure: Finding a source
of stress management. *NASSP Bulletin, 97*(4), 335-349.

Weiler, L. D., Jr. (2001). Department heads The most underutilized leadership
position. NASSP Bulletin, 85(625), 73-81. doi:10.1177/019263650108562508

Werner, E. E. & Smith, R. S. (1992). Overcoming the odds: high-risk children
from birth to adulthood. Ithaca, NY: Cornell University Press.

What Is Dyscalculia? What Should I Do If My Child Has It? (n.d.). Retrieved from
https://www.webmd.com/add-adhd/childhood-adhd/dyscalculia-facts

What is an Individual Health Care Plan (IHCP)? (2019, January 9). Retrieved
from https://www.educare.co.uk/news/what-is-an-individual-health-care-plan

What is low vision? (n.d.). Https://Www.Allaboutvision.Com/Lowvision/.
Retrieved March 6, 2021, from https://www.allaboutvision.com/lowvision/

Wheatley, M.D. (2012). Cultural Intelligence for Leaders. Creative Commons.
Retrieved 7/2019 2012. https://2012books.lardbucket.org/pdfs/cultural-
intelligence-for-leaders.pdf

Whitaker, M. & Ortiz, S. (2019). What a Specific Learning Disability Is Not:
Examining Exclusionary Factors. National Center for Learning Disabilities-White
Paper. Retrieved from: https://www.ncld.org/wp-
content/uploads/2019/11/What-a-Specific-Learning-Disability-Is-Not-
Examining-Exclusionary-Factors.12192019.pdf

Whitaker, T. (2003). What great principals do differently: Fifteen things that
matter most. Routledge.

Whitener, E. M., Brodt, S. E., Korsgaard, M. A., & Werner, J. M. (1998).
Managers as initiators of trust: An exchange relationship framework for
understanding trustworthy managerial behavior. Academy of management
review, 23(3), 513-530.

Why It's Important That We Study History? (n.d.).
https://www.arcadiapublishing.com/Navigation/Community/Arcadia-and-THP-Blog/June-2016/Why-It%E2%80%99s-Important-That-We-Study-History

Wikipedia contributors. (n.d.). DSM-5. Retrieved from
https://en.wikipedia.org/wiki/DSM-5

Wingspread (2004). Declaration on school connections. Journal of School Health, 74(7), 233–234

Yate, M. (2009). Hiring the best: A manager's guide to effective interviewing and recruiting. Cincinnati, OH: F & W Media.

Yell, M. L., Rogers, D., & Rogers, E. L. (1998). The legal history of special education: What a long, strange trip it's been!. Remedial and special education, 19(4), 219-228.

Yell, M. L., Drasgow, E., Bradley, R., & Justesen, T. (2004). Contemporary legal issues in special education. In A. McCray Sorrells, H. Rieth, & P. T. Sindelar (Eds.), Critical issues in special education (pp. 16-36). Boston: Pearson Education.

Zanderer, D. G. (1992). Integrity: An essential Executive quality. Business Forum, Fall, 12-16

Zirkel, P. (1997). Blurring the lines between special and regular education. In Section

504 compliance: Issues, analysis, and cases (pp 17-19). Horsham, PA: LRP Publications

Amended References

Alberto P.A, Troutman A.C. 2009. *Applied behavior analysis for teachers (8th ed.)* Upper Saddle River, NJ: Pearson

The Advocacy Institute (n.d.). Section 504 stats

Carr, E. G., Horner, R. H., Turnbull, A. P., Marquis, J. G., Magito-McLaughlin, D., McAtee, M. L., Smith, C. E., Ryan, K. A., Ruef, M. B., & Doolabh, A. (1997). Positive behavioral support as an approach for dealing with problem behavior in people with developmental disabilities: A research synthesis. Unpublished manuscript, State University of New York, Stony Brook.

Carr, E. G., Levin, L., McConnachie, G., Carlson, J. I., Kemp, D. C. & Smith, C. E. (1994). Communication-based intervention for problem behavior: A user's guide for producing positive change. Baltimore: Brookes.

Civil rights data | U.S. Department of Education. (n.d.).
https://civilrightsdata.ed.gov/estimations/2017-2018

Coates, R. D. (1989). The Regular Education Initiative and opinions of regular classroom teachers. Journal of Learning Disabilities, 22, 532-536. The discipline problem--And ways to deal with it. (1996,October). CEC Today, 3(4), 1-5.

Disability Legislation History - Student Disability Center. (2023, May 24). Student Disability Center. https://disabilitycenter.colostate.edu/disability-awareness/disability-history/#:~:text=The%20Rehabilitation%20Act%20was%20the,the%20legal%20support%20established%20in

Duke, D. L. (1990). School organization, leadership, and student behavior. *Student discipline strategies: Research and practice,* 19-46.

Educational Studies, 19, 91-105. O'Neill, R. E., Horner, R. H., Albin, R. A., Sprague, J. R., Storey, K., & Newton, J. S. (1997). Functional assessment and program development for problem behavior: A practical handbook. Pacific Grove, CA: Brooks/Cole.

Essential components of MTSS | Center on Multi-Tiered Systems of Support. (n.d.). https://mtss4success.org/essential-components

Elam, S., Rose, L., & Gallup, A. (1996). Twenty-eighth annual Phi Delta Kappa/Gallup poll of the public's attitudes toward the public schools. Phi Delta Kappan, 78, 41- 59.
Sugai, G., Lewis-Palmer, T., & Hagan-Burke, S. (2000). Overview of the functional behavioral assessment process. *Exceptionality, 8*(3), 149-160.

Ferro, J., Foster-Johnson, L., & Dunlap, G. (1996). Relation between curricular activities and problem behaviors of students with mental retardation. *American Journal of Mental Retardation: AJMR, 101*(2), 184-194. Tomlinson, C. A. (2000a). The Differentiated Classroom: Responding to the Needs of all Learners. Alexandria: Association for Supervision and Curriculum Development.

Fundamentals of SEL - CASEL. (2023, June 29). CASEL. https://casel.org/fundamentals-of-sel/

Gartner, A., & Lipsky, D.K. (1987). Beyond special education:Toward a quality system for all students. Harvard Educational Review, 57, 367-395.

Guest. (2023). The benefits of Self-Management Skills in Coaching techniques. *NovoEd.* https://novoed.com/resources/blog/self-management-and-coaching/

Hall, T. (2002). Differentiated Instruction. Effective Classroom Practices Report, National Center on Accessing the General Curriculum, Office of Special Education Programs, U.S. Department of Education

Horner, R. H., Albin, R. W., & O'Neill, R. E. (1996). Supporting students with severe intellectual disabilities and severe challenging behaviors. In G. Stoner, M. R. Shinn, & H. M. Walker (Eds.), Interventions for achievement and behavior problems (pp. 269-288). Bethesda, MD: National Association of School Psychologists.

Horner, R. H., & Diemer, S. M. (1992). Educational support for students with severe problem behaviors in Oregon: A descriptive analysis from the 1987-1988 school year. Journal of the Association for Persons with Severe Handicaps, 17, 154-169

Lannie, A. L., & McCurdy, B. L. (2007). Preventing disruptive behavior in the urban classroom: Effects of the good behavior game on student and teacher behavior. *Education and Treatment of children, 30*(1), 85-98.

Lannie, A. L., & McCurdy, B. L. (2007). Preventing disruptive behavior in the urban classroom: Effects of the good behavior game on student and teacher behavior. *Education and Treatment of children, 30*(1), 85-98.

Losen, D. J., Hodson, C. L., Keith II, M. A., Morrison, K., & Belway, S. (2015). Are we closing the school discipline gap?.

Lewis, T., Sugai, G., & Colvin, G. (1998). Reducing problem behavior through a schoolwise system of effective behavioral support: Investigation of a school-wide social skills training program and contextual interventions. School Psychology Review, 27, 446-459.

Madsen, C. K., & Duke, R. A. (1987). The Effect of Teacher Training on the Ability to Recognize Need for Giving Approval for Appropriate Student Behavior. *Bulletin of the Council for Research in Music Education, 91*, 103–109. http://www.jstor.org/stable/40318069

Merrett, F., & Wheldall, K. (1993). How do teachers learn to manage classroom behavior? A study of teachers' opinions about their initial training with special reference to classroom behavior management.

MURDOCK SR, D. P. (2007). School-wide behavioral support: A theory-based program implementation study of Positive Behavioral Interventions and Support (Doctoral dissertation, University of Cincinnati).

Ruef, M. B., Higgins, C., Glaeser, B. J. C., & Patnode, M. (1998). Positive Behavioral Support: Strategies for teachers. *Intervention in School and Clinic, 34*(1), 21–32. https://doi.org/10.1177/105345129803400103

Neal, C. (2015). When five hours equals five days: Bringing section 504 education plans into the 21st century. *North Carolina Journal of Law & Technology, 16*(5), 235.

Snell, M. E., & Brown, F. (1993). Instructional planning and implementation. In M. E. Snell (Ed.), Instruction of students with severe disabilities (4th ed., pp. 99-151). New York: Macmillan.

Sugai, G., & Horner, R. H. (1994). Including students with severe behavior problems in general education settings: Assumptions, challenges, and solutions. In J. Marr, G. Sugai, & G. Tindal (Eds.), The Oregon Conference Monograph, 6, 109-120.

Taylor-Greene, S., Brown, D., Nelson, L., Longton, J., Gassman, T., Cohen, J., ... & Hall, S. (1997). School-wide behavioral support: Starting the year off right. Journal of Behavioral Education, 7, 99-112.

Tomlinson, C. A. (2000b). Reconciliable differences. Educational Leadership, 58(1), 6-11.

Tomlinson, C. A. (2001a). Differentiated instruction in the regular classroom. Understanding Our Gifted, 14(1), 3-6.

Tomlinson, C. A. (2001b). Grading for success. Educational Leadership, 58(6), 12-15.

Tomlinson, C. A. (2001c). How to Differentiate Instruction in Mixed-Ability Classrooms (2nd ed.). Alexandria: Association for Supervision and Curriculum Development.

Tomlinson, C. A. (2002). Different learners different lessons. Instructor, 112(2), 21-25.

Tomlinson, C. A. (2003). Deciding to teach them all. Educational Leadership, 61(2), 6-11.

Tomlinson, C. A. (2004a). Differentiation in diverse settings. School Administrator, 61(7), 28-33.

Tomlinson, C. A. (2004b). Research evidence for differentiation. School Administrator, 61(7), 30.

Tomlinson, C. A. (2004c). Sharing responsibility for differentiating instruction. Roeper Review, 26(4), 188-200.

Wallace Jr, J. M., Goodkind, S., Wallace, C. M., & Bachman, J. G. (2008). Racial, ethnic, and gender differences in school discipline among US high school students: 1991-2005. *The Negro educational review, 59*(1-2), 47.

Yael Cannon, Michael Gregory & Julie Waterstone, A Solution Hiding in Plain Sight: Special Education and Better Outcomes for Students with Social, Emotional and Behavioral Challenges, 41 Fordham Urb. L.J. 403 (2013).

DR. NAKIA S. COTTON